Clinical Intelligence for Mass Tort Litigation™

How the Lexcura Clinical Intelligence Model™ Identifies Stronger Cases, Reduces Risk, and Improves Litigation Outcomes

Lexcura Summit

"Clinical Intelligence for Mass Tort Litigation," "Lexcura Clinical Intelligence Model," and "Clinical Intelligence Command Center" are trademarks of Lexcura Summit.

This book is intended to provide general information regarding mass tort litigation practice and the Lexcura Clinical Intelligence Model. It does not constitute legal advice, medical advice, or a guarantee of any particular litigation or business outcome. Readers should consult qualified counsel and clinical professionals regarding their specific circumstances.

ISBN: 979-8-9973079-6-7 (Paperback)

ISBN: 979-8-9973079-5-0 (Hardcover)

Dedication

To every person whose individual story became one claim among thousands.

To the families who have waited for answers, the attorneys responsible for finding them, and the clinicians whose knowledge helps reveal what the records alone cannot explain.

Mass tort litigation is necessarily conducted at scale, but injury is never experienced at scale. It is experienced by one person, within one body, through one sequence of events, and with consequences that are entirely their own.

This book is dedicated to those who believe that efficiency must never replace accuracy, that volume must never obscure truth, and that every claimant deserves to be evaluated as an individual.

May better clinical intelligence lead to stronger decisions, more defensible claims, and a fairer path to justice.

Preface

Mass tort litigation presents a challenge unlike almost any other area of legal practice.

Thousands of individuals may allege injury arising from the same drug, device, chemical, product, or exposure. Their claims may appear similar at first, yet the clinical realities behind them can be profoundly different. Each claimant brings a separate medical history, a different baseline, a distinct pattern of exposure, and an individual sequence of diagnoses, treatment decisions, complications, and outcomes.

The scale of the litigation demands efficiency. The integrity of the process demands something more.

It demands clinical intelligence.

Too often, mass tort review begins with the assumption that a shared exposure creates a shared clinical story. It does not. Exposure may establish a common point of inquiry, but it does not establish injury. A diagnosis does not automatically establish causation. Temporal association does not prove that one event caused another. A claimant may have the alleged injury but lack sufficient evidence of exposure. Another may have documented exposure but no clinically verifiable injury. A third may meet both criteria but have competing medical factors that materially affect causation.

These distinctions determine the strength, value, and defensibility of a claim.

They cannot be identified reliably through document collection alone.

For more than four decades, I have worked within healthcare and examined the relationship between clinical events, medical documentation, professional decision-making, and patient outcomes. That experience taught me that a medical record is not a ready-made explanation of what happened. It is a fragmented account created by different professionals, at different times, for different purposes.

The relevant clinical story must be reconstructed.

In mass tort litigation, that reconstruction must also be repeatable. A review process cannot depend entirely on the individual judgment of one reviewer or change according to who happens to examine the file. It must apply consistent standards across the claimant population while retaining the ability to identify what is clinically unique about each person.

That is the purpose of this book.

The mass tort clinical intelligence methodology presented here provides a disciplined structure for moving from claimant intake to litigation-ready analysis. It examines six essential stages:

Record Ingestion

Establishes whether the necessary documentation has been obtained and whether the record is sufficiently complete to support review.

Exposure Mapping

Determines whether the alleged product, drug, device, substance, or environmental factor can be reliably connected to the claimant.

Injury Verification

Establishes whether the claimed condition is supported by objective clinical evidence rather than allegation, coding, or diagnosis language alone.

Causation Analysis

Evaluates whether the exposure is medically and temporally capable of producing the alleged injury while identifying alternative causes, confounding conditions, and evidentiary limitations.

Claimant Classification

Organizes claims according to clinical strength, completeness, complexity, and litigation relevance.

Bellwether and Expert Escalation

Identifies the claims requiring deeper specialist review, expert analysis, deposition preparation, or strategic consideration.

These stages are not designed merely to accelerate review. Speed without reliability creates greater risk. The purpose is to make large-scale review more consistent, transparent, auditable, and clinically defensible.

This methodology also recognizes an essential truth: mass tort litigation involves both a population and a person.

Population-level evidence can identify patterns, associations, and potential risk. It can help establish general causation and explain why a product or exposure warrants investigation. It cannot, by itself, establish what happened to an individual claimant. That requires examination of the claimant's baseline health, exposure history, latency period, clinical progression, diagnostic evidence, treatment course, competing risk factors, and outcome.

The legal team and the clinical team therefore cannot operate as separate disciplines reviewing the same case from opposite sides. They must work together.

Attorneys understand the legal theory, procedural requirements, evidentiary burdens, and strategic objectives of the litigation. Clinicians understand disease processes, medical plausibility, diagnostic reasoning, treatment decisions, and the significance of what appears — or fails to appear — in the record. Neither perspective is sufficient in isolation.

Clinical intelligence creates the bridge between them.

This book has been written for attorneys, clinical reviewers, legal nurse consultants, healthcare experts, litigation teams, claims administrators, and organizations responsible for evaluating mass tort claims at scale. It is intended to provide a common structure through which legal and clinical professionals can examine the same evidence, ask better questions, and reach more informed conclusions.

The objective is not to prove every claim.

Nor is it to dismiss claims simply because the records are complex, incomplete, or difficult to interpret.

The objective is to determine, as accurately and consistently as possible, what the available evidence supports.

Strong claims should be recognized early and developed appropriately. Unsupported claims should be identified before they consume disproportionate resources or weaken the credibility of the wider litigation. Incomplete claims should be distinguished from clinically deficient ones so that missing evidence can be pursued rather than mistaken for an absence of merit. Complex claims should be escalated to the appropriate level of expertise instead of being forced through a standardized process that cannot adequately evaluate them.

When this work is performed properly, mass tort review becomes more than a screening exercise. It becomes a clinically governed system of evidence evaluation.

That is the standard this book seeks to establish.

Because behind every claimant number is an individual medical story.

And that story deserves to be understood before a legal conclusion is reached.

Michelle Carroll

Founder & CEO, Lexcura Summit

Introduction: Why Mass Tort Litigation Needs Clinical Intelligence

Mass tort litigation is built on a premise that sounds simple and turns out to be extraordinarily difficult to execute: many people were harmed by the same exposure, in similar ways, and their claims can be pursued together with more efficiency and more leverage than any one of them could achieve alone. The premise is sound. The execution is where firms struggle, because "similar" is doing an enormous amount of work in that sentence, and the only way to know whether a given claimant's case is truly similar — medically, temporally, causally — is to read their records with the same rigor a solo practitioner would bring to a single, career-defining case.

Most firms cannot do that at scale, not because they lack competence, but because the traditional model of medical record review was never built for the volumes mass tort litigation now produces. A firm managing a few dozen personal injury cases can afford a thorough, individualized review of every file. A firm managing several thousand mass tort claimants cannot apply that same depth of review to every claimant without either bankrupting the litigation budget or slowing case development to a pace that costs the firm its most valuable inventory: time.

The result, across the industry, is a familiar and expensive pattern. Firms acquire claimants in volume, apply a shallow, largely administrative review at intake, and only discover the real clinical strength or weakness of a case much later — sometimes not until a bellwether selection process, sometimes not until the defense's own medical experts do the work the firm never did. By then, the firm has already spent years of litigation capital, attorney time, and expert fees on an inventory it never actually understood.

This book introduces Clinical Intelligence as the discipline that closes that gap. It is not a faster way to summarize medical records, and it is not simply an outsourced review service. It is a structured methodology for determining what medical evidence actually supports — for a single claimant and for an entire portfolio — early enough that the answer can still change the firm's strategy, not just document its history.

The chapters that follow move through a deliberate sequence. Part I establishes why the existing mass tort review model is no longer sufficient at current claim volumes. Part II introduces the Lexcura Clinical Intelligence Model™ itself, built on seven analytical pillars that move from record integrity through causation mapping. Part III applies that model across an entire claimant portfolio, showing how tiered review and structured classification let a firm allocate its most expensive resources — senior clinical reviewers, specialists, retained experts — only where they are actually needed. Part IV makes the economic case directly, translating clinical rigor into the language of cost per claimant, portfolio return, and avoided expenditure. Part V connects the methodology to the specific moments where it matters most in active litigation: bellwether selection, discovery, expert strategy, and settlement. Part VI addresses how to operationalize all of this at enterprise scale, including the appropriate role — and appropriate limits — of artificial intelligence in a clinically governed review process. Part VII closes by arguing that the firms who will lead mass tort litigation over the next decade will not be the firms with the largest inventories, but the firms who can tell, earlier and more reliably than anyone else, what their inventories actually mean.

How to Use This Book

A note on structure before you begin. The Preface describes this methodology at the level firm leadership needs first: six stages, moving from Record Ingestion through Bellwether and Expert Escalation. Part II of this book goes one level deeper, breaking the analytical work inside those six stages into seven pillars — because a single stage like Causation Analysis, for example, actually draws on several distinct disciplines (standard of care review, regulatory overlay, and causation mapping specifically) that deserve to be taught separately even though they serve one stage of the larger process. Chapter 13's pipeline goes deeper still, into the operational sequence a claimant file physically moves through. These three views are not competing methodologies. They are the same discipline described at three levels of resolution: the Preface's six stages are the executive summary, the seven pillars are the analytical curriculum, and the pipeline is the operating procedure. Roughly speaking, Record Ingestion corresponds to the record integrity pillar; Exposure Mapping and Injury Verification draw on baseline profiling, imaging analysis, and timeline reconstruction; Causation Analysis draws on standard of care review, the regulatory overlay, and causation mapping together; and Claimant Classification and Bellwether and Expert Escalation correspond directly to the classification and escalation stages described throughout Parts III and V.

This book is written for two overlapping audiences, and it is worth naming both so you can read it accordingly.

The first audience is the litigation team — attorneys, case managers, and clinical reviewers — who need a working methodology they can apply to actual claimant files. For that audience, Parts II, III, and V are the operational core of the book, and the appendices are designed to be used directly: as checklists, as classification frameworks, as templates to adapt to your own tort and your own firm.

The second audience is firm leadership — managing partners, CFOs, and litigation funders — who need to understand Clinical Intelligence not as a review technique but as a capital allocation decision. For that audience, Part IV translates the methodology directly into the economic terms that justify enterprise adoption, and Chapter 24 in particular is written to be shared directly with decision-makers who may never read the rest of the book.

Most readers will move through the book in order, since each part builds on the one before it. But if your firm already has a mature review process and you are evaluating whether Clinical Intelligence is worth adopting, you may want to begin with Part IV, confirm the economic case for yourself, and then return to Part II to understand the methodology that produces those numbers.

The appendices are also not uniform in kind, and it is worth knowing which is which before relying on them. Appendix A, Appendix H, and Appendix I are worked examples, built directly from the composite claimants used throughout this book, and are meant to show the methodology applied to something close to an actual file. The remaining appendices — B, C, E, F, G, J, and K — are adaptable templates: starting frameworks built to be populated with your own firm's criteria, evidence thresholds, and tort-specific detail, not filled-in examples in their own right.

PART I

I

The Mass Tort Problem

Why the existing mass tort review model is no longer sufficient.

Chapter 1 — The Scale Problem in Mass Tort Litigation

A mass tort firm does not manage one medically complex case. It manages hundreds, thousands, or tens of thousands of claimants, each carrying a different medical history, a different exposure profile, a different injury presentation, and a different causation pathway — and each of those differences matters to how the case should ultimately be valued, litigated, or declined. That plurality is the entire premise of mass tort practice, and it is also the source of nearly every operational failure this book will describe.

Consider what a single claimant file actually requires. A complete medical-legal review means collecting records across every treating provider, reconciling gaps and inconsistencies between them, establishing what the claimant's health looked like before the alleged exposure, tracing the timeline of symptoms and diagnosis against the exposure period, and forming a defensible view of whether the claimed injury is more likely explained by the exposure or by something else entirely. Done properly, for one claimant, that is real clinical and legal work — the kind a solo practitioner might spend dozens of hours on for a single case worth pursuing.

Multiply that by a claimant inventory in the thousands, and the arithmetic stops working. No firm has the attorney hours, the clinical reviewer capacity, or the expert budget to apply that same depth of review to every claimant on day one. And yet the pressure to make acquisition and investment decisions does not wait for a thorough review to catch up — intake continues, marketing spend continues, and decisions about which claimants to pursue, invest in, and prioritize get made anyway, often on far thinner information than the firm would like to admit.

This is not simply a resourcing problem that more hiring could solve. Mass tort intake is typically driven by advertising and referral pipelines built to generate volume, and that intake engine runs on its own schedule, largely independent of how quickly clinical review can actually process what it produces. A campaign that generates several hundred new claimant inquiries in a month does not pause while the firm catches up on reviewing the several hundred it received the month before. Firms that do not anticipate this mismatch end up making a quiet, usually unstated trade: either intake slows to match review capacity, which most firms are reluctant to do once a campaign is generating leads, or review depth quietly erodes to match intake volume, which is the far more common outcome and the one this book is written to prevent.

This creates several predictable and expensive symptoms, all of which will recur throughout this book:

Figure 1.1 — Undifferentiated review at scale produces the same recurring set of symptoms, regardless of firm size.

The firm applies inconsistent screening. Because there is no standardized method for determining clinical strength at intake, different reviewers — or the same reviewer under different time pressure — reach different conclusions about similar claimants. A case that would have been flagged as weak by one reviewer sails through under another.

Review capacity becomes the bottleneck, not case merit. Strong claims wait in the same queue as weak ones, because the firm has no reliable way to identify which claimants deserve early attention until everyone has been reviewed at roughly the same level.

The firm defaults to reviewing every case at the same depth, which is simultaneously too much for the weakest claimants and not enough for the strongest ones. A claimant who should have been screened out in an afternoon consumes the same review resources as a claimant who deserves a senior clinical reviewer's full attention.

Identification of the portfolio's strongest cases is delayed, sometimes for years, because there is no structured way to surface them early. Meanwhile, weak claims — the ones with real causation problems, missing records, or pre-existing conditions that undermine the claimed injury — remain in the inventory far longer than they should, quietly consuming record-retrieval costs, review hours, and attorney attention that could have gone toward stronger cases.

Comparing claimants to one another becomes difficult or impossible, because without a standardized clinical framework, "strong" and "weak" mean whatever the individual reviewer who happened to look at the file decided they meant. This makes portfolio-level decisions — which claimants to prioritize, which to escalate to experts, which to consider for bellwether selection — much harder to defend later, whether to firm leadership, to a litigation funder, or to opposing counsel testing the firm's process in discovery.

Incomplete or inaccurate underlying data compounds every one of these problems. When a firm does not have a rigorous, standardized method for reviewing what it has, it also has no reliable way to know what it is missing — which records have not been obtained, which claimants have gaps that will surface as vulnerabilities later, and which conclusions were reached based on incomplete information.

It is worth being clear about why this problem is qualitatively different from anything a solo practitioner or small personal injury firm encounters, rather than simply a bigger version of the same challenge. A solo practitioner handling a dozen complex cases can hold the details of each one in working memory, notice when something about a file feels inconsistent with what they would expect, and apply that instinct consistently because the same person is applying it every time. That kind of tacit, accumulated clinical judgment does not scale to a review team of twenty or fifty people processing thousands of files, no matter how experienced any individual reviewer is. What worked as an individual habit has to become an explicit, documented methodology the moment more than one person is applying it — and most firms never make that translation deliberately. They simply hope that hiring experienced reviewers will reproduce, informally and at scale, judgment that was never actually standardized in the first place.

The chapter, and the argument this entire book will make, rests on a single principle worth stating plainly before moving further: mass tort litigation is not merely a volume problem. It is a clinical intelligence problem operating at scale. The firms that treat it only as a volume problem — solved by adding more reviewers, more administrative staff, more processing capacity — will keep running into the same wall, because more people applying an unstructured review process simply produces more inconsistency, faster. The firms that recognize it as a clinical intelligence problem, and build a methodology capable of operating at claimant-portfolio scale, are the ones who will actually close the gap between how many claimants they have and how well they understand them.

Chapter 2 — Why Traditional Medical Record Review Is Not Enough

Ask a mass tort firm whether its claimants' medical records have been reviewed, and the honest answer is almost always yes. Ask whether the firm knows what those records mean for the litigation, and the honest answer is far less certain. That gap between reviewed and understood is the subject of this chapter, and it is one of the most consequential — and least discussed — problems in mass tort practice.

The confusion exists because "medical record review" is treated as a single activity, when it is actually a chain of distinct analytical steps, each of which can be done well or badly, and each of which produces something different:

Record retrieval is the collection of the documents themselves — obtaining what exists from providers, pharmacies, and facilities. It answers the question of what documentation is available, not what it means.

Data extraction is the process of pulling discrete facts out of those documents — dates, diagnoses, medications, providers — typically into a structured or semi-structured format. It produces raw material for analysis, not analysis itself.

A medical chronology arranges those extracted facts into a timeline. It is genuinely useful, and genuinely necessary, but a chronology is descriptive, not evaluative. It tells you what happened and roughly when.

A medical summary goes a step further, condensing the chronology into a narrative a non-clinician can read. This is where many firms — and many outsourced review vendors — stop, and it is precisely where the real analytical work has not yet begun.

Clinical interpretation asks what the medical facts actually mean in context: whether findings are consistent with the claimed injury, whether a diagnosis is well supported by objective evidence or largely a clinical impression, whether the severity documented in the records matches the severity being claimed.

Causation analysis goes further still, asking whether the exposure at issue is a plausible explanation for the claimant's condition, what alternative explanations exist, and how strong the temporal and biological relationship actually is.

Litigation intelligence is the final step: converting all of the above into something an attorney can actually use — a defensible classification of case strength, a clear statement of what evidence supports and undermines the claim, and a recommendation about how the firm should invest its resources in this particular claimant.

This chain matters because the vendors and services many firms rely on to manage volume are, almost without exception, built to excel at the earlier steps and stop well short of the later ones. A record-retrieval vendor is measured on how completely and quickly it obtains documents, not on whether those documents support a viable claim. A medical chronology or summary service is measured on turnaround time and readability, not on whether it flags a competing cause the firm has not yet considered. None of this is a criticism of those services on their own terms — they generally do what they are built to do, efficiently and at scale. The problem is a firm that treats a completed chronology, purchased from a vendor built to produce chronologies, as though it were a completed clinical intelligence review. The vendor delivered exactly what it promised. The firm simply asked the wrong question of it.

Most mass tort review processes stop somewhere around the chronology or summary stage and treat that as equivalent to a complete review. It is not. A chronology can show, accurately and in perfect chronological order, that a claimant was diagnosed with a condition during the relevant exposure period — and still leave every question that actually matters to the litigation unanswered.

A chronology alone does not establish whether the condition was pre-existing, documented years before the exposure began under a different or related diagnosis. It does not establish whether the claimed injury is objectively supported by imaging, pathology, or laboratory findings, or whether it rests primarily on the claimant's self-reported symptoms and a treating physician's clinical impression. It does not establish whether the timing between exposure and diagnosis is medically plausible given what is known about latency for that condition, or whether it falls outside a biologically reasonable window. It does not identify whether another cause — a documented comorbidity, a competing exposure, an unrelated disease process — is in fact the more likely explanation. It does not flag whether critical records are simply missing, leaving the firm's understanding of the claimant incomplete in ways that will surface, unfavorably, in discovery. It does not assess whether the claimant's case, as documented, is likely to withstand focused defense scrutiny. And it does not answer the question that actually drives resource allocation: whether this particular claim, given everything the records show, warrants additional investment.

Firms that rely on chronology-level review and treat it as a finished analysis are, in effect, making litigation and financial decisions based on what is written in the record rather than what the record establishes. Those are not the same thing, and the distance between them is exactly where mass tort portfolios accumulate risk. Closing that distance — moving reliably from record to meaning — is the purpose of the methodology introduced in Part II.

In Practice: A composite hair-relaxer claimant, alleging that decades of product use contributed to a uterine cancer diagnosis, shows how far a chronology-level review can miss the actual question. A chronology built from this claimant's intake questionnaire would accurately record "reports using hair relaxers regularly since adolescence" — and stop there, as though the sentence itself were exposure evidence. It is not. Brand and formulation, frequency of use, and any purchase or salon records behind that statement are what turn a self-reported history into something a causation analysis can actually rely on. A firm that treats the questionnaire response as equivalent to verified exposure has not finished the review; it has stopped at the point where the real work begins.

Chapter 3 — The Cost of Clinical Uncertainty

Every chapter so far has argued that shallow medical record review creates analytical blind spots. This chapter puts a different lens on the same problem: what those blind spots actually cost, in dollars and in litigation capital, when they are allowed to persist across a large claimant portfolio.

The costs are not limited to the obvious ones. Acquiring unsuitable cases is the most visible cost, and the easiest for firm leadership to recognize once it happens — a claimant taken on without adequate clinical screening turns out, months or years later, to have a fatal causation problem that could have been identified at intake. But the more expensive costs are usually the quieter, cumulative ones that never show up as a single bad decision.

Carrying a weak claim for several years is expensive in ways that compound. The claim continues to consume record-retrieval costs as additional providers are identified. It continues to be touched by staff during periodic file reviews and status updates. If it survives long enough to reach an expert referral, it consumes expert budget that a stronger claimant could have used more productively — and worse, if the weakness was never properly identified, the expert may spend billable hours reaching a conclusion the firm's own review process should have surfaced far earlier.

Repeated review of the same records is a specific and common form of this waste. Without a standardized, documented review process, the same claimant file is often examined multiple times by different people — an initial intake reviewer, a case manager checking status, an attorney preparing for a discovery deadline — each starting close to from scratch because there is no reliable, shared record of what a prior review already established.

Ordering unnecessary expert reviews follows the same pattern at a much higher price point. When a firm cannot distinguish, internally, between a claimant with a genuinely difficult causation question and a claimant whose weakness could have been identified through more careful record review, it tends to default to sending both types of cases to retained experts. Expert time is among the most expensive resources in mass tort litigation, and using it to answer questions the firm's own clinical review should have already answered is one of the most avoidable costs in the entire system.

Failing to obtain decisive records early creates a different kind of cost — one measured in delay rather than dollars, though the delay eventually becomes a dollar cost too. A missing operative report or a missing set of prior imaging can leave a claimant's causation picture genuinely unresolved for years, not because the answer is unknowable, but because no one flagged, early enough, that the record existed and needed to be obtained.

For firms that finance their litigation costs — whether through a litigation funder, a line of credit, or internal capital that has an opportunity cost of its own — every one of these delays carries an additional layer of expense that rarely gets attributed back to the review process that caused it. Capital carrying a claimant for an extra eighteen months while a decisive record sits unrequested is capital that is not available for a stronger claimant elsewhere in the portfolio, and it is accruing financing cost the entire time. Firms that track their overall cost of capital closely, but do not connect that cost back to review-process delays at the individual claimant level, are missing one of the more direct financial arguments for adopting a more disciplined intake and review process in the first place.

Missing valuable claims within a large inventory may be the most costly failure of all, because it is invisible. A firm that cannot reliably surface its strongest claimants early is not just failing those claimants — it is failing to direct settlement negotiations, bellwether strategy, and litigation resources toward the cases that could most improve the entire portfolio's outcome. An inventory of five thousand claimants likely contains a meaningful number of exceptionally strong cases. If the review process cannot find them until very late in the litigation, the firm has effectively been managing its portfolio blind for years.

Selecting poor bellwether candidates compounds this problem at the worst possible moment. Bellwether trials are meant to test the strength of a representative slice of the inventory, and a poorly selected bellwether — one that looked adequate on a superficial review but collapses under focused defense scrutiny — can damage settlement leverage for the entire portfolio, not just for that one claimant.

Discovering causation weaknesses late, rather than at intake or early review, means the firm learns about a claimant's fatal flaw at the worst possible time to learn it: often during discovery, sometimes not until the defense's own experts identify it. By then, the firm has already spent years of resources treating the claim as viable.

Applying inconsistent review standards across the portfolio — the natural result of not having a standardized methodology — makes every one of these problems worse and harder to manage, because the firm cannot even reliably compare its own claimants to one another, let alone defend its portfolio decisions to a funder, a co-counsel, or a court.

And underlying all of it is the simplest failure of all: treating every claimant as though the case has equal value and equal risk, when in reality, within any large mass tort inventory, claimants vary enormously in clinical strength, evidentiary completeness, and litigation readiness. A review process that does not differentiate between them is not neutral — it is actively obscuring the differences that should be driving the firm's most important resource decisions.

Taken together, these costs describe a portfolio being managed without the clinical intelligence needed to manage it well. The next section of this book introduces the methodology built specifically to close that gap: not a faster version of traditional record review, but a structured discipline for determining what the evidence actually establishes, early enough and consistently enough to change how the firm invests, litigates, and negotiates.

PART II

II

The Lexcura Clinical Intelligence Model

An integrated analytical methodology, not a series of isolated review tasks.

Figure 2.1 — The Lexcura Clinical Intelligence Model: seven analytical pillars feeding a litigation-ready output.

Chapter 4 — From Medical Information to Clinical Intelligence

Clinical Intelligence, as this book uses the term, is the disciplined interpretation of medical information within its clinical, temporal, evidentiary, regulatory, and legal context. That definition is deliberately dense, because each of those five contexts answers a question a plain medical summary leaves open. The clinical context asks whether a finding is medically significant or incidental. The temporal context asks whether the sequence of events is biologically plausible. The evidentiary context asks whether a claim is objectively supported or merely asserted. The regulatory context asks whether the exposure occurred under conditions the law recognizes as actionable. The legal context asks what all of the above actually means for the claim being made.

The Lexcura Clinical Intelligence Model did not emerge from a desire to summarize records more efficiently. It emerged from a smaller, more persistent set of questions, asked case after case, that traditional review consistently failed to answer: What is missing from this file? What does the evidence actually establish, as opposed to what the claimant's narrative assumes? What has been assumed without being documented? What alternative explanation exists for this presentation? Does the timeline actually support the alleged sequence of cause and effect? Is the injury objectively demonstrated, or does it rest on subjective report? What will the defense identify the moment they receive this file? And, most practically, what additional information would actually change how this case should be assessed?

Those eight questions are not a checklist to complete once and set aside. They are the recurring discipline underneath everything in Part II. The seven pillars that follow — record integrity, baseline profiling, imaging analysis, timeline reconstruction, standard of care review, regulatory and compliance overlay, and causation mapping — are simply the structured application of those questions to the specific categories of evidence a mass tort claimant file contains.

It is worth being explicit about what this model is not. It is not a faster medical chronology. A chronology can be produced by extracting dates and events without ever asking whether the sequence is medically plausible or whether a competing explanation is more likely. It is not a substitute for expert opinion where a genuine, complex causation question requires one. And it is not a scoring algorithm that replaces professional judgment with a number. It is, instead, the structured groundwork that makes expert time more productive, that makes professional judgment more consistent across a large team, and that ensures the questions an expert or opposing counsel will eventually ask have already been asked — and answered as well as the record allows — long before they are asked by someone outside the firm.

It is also worth being explicit about who actually applies this model, because the answer shapes everything in the chapters that follow. The underlying clinical analysis should be performed by appropriately trained clinical reviewers — nurse consultants, physician assistants, or similarly credentialed staff — working under defined protocols and with a clear escalation path to supervising clinicians or retained experts for the questions that genuinely require their judgment. The attorney's role is different but equally essential: defining the legally material questions, protecting the procedural and evidentiary framework, and converting the clinical findings into litigation decisions — the subject of Part VIII of this book. Firms that ask attorneys to perform the clinical analysis themselves are usually paying attorney rates for clinical-review work, and getting a less rigorous clinical review in the bargain.

Chapter 5 — Pillar One: Record Integrity

Before a claimant can be meaningfully assessed, the firm has to know whether the evidentiary record in front of it is complete and reliable enough to support an assessment at all. Record integrity is the first pillar precisely because every other pillar depends on it — a causation analysis built on an incomplete or unreliable record is not a weaker analysis, it is an unreliable one, however sound the reasoning applied to it.

In a mass tort context, record integrity problems take on a specific, recurring shape. Missing provider records are the most common: a claimant's own account of their treatment history frequently references providers whose records were never obtained, leaving gaps the firm may not even be aware exist until much later. Missing diagnostic studies and missing pharmacy histories create similar blind spots, particularly when they would otherwise establish or undercut a baseline condition. Incomplete exposure records — proof of purchase, prescription history, occupational documentation — can leave the exposure element of the claim itself under-supported, independent of any question about the injury.

Duplicate and conflicting documents are a quieter but equally serious problem: the same encounter appearing twice with different details, or two providers documenting the same period in ways that do not reconcile, both of which can create false confidence in either direction if they are not identified and resolved. Gaps in treatment — periods where a claimant with an allegedly ongoing condition has no documented care — deserve the same scrutiny, since an unexplained gap can undermine both the injury claim and its severity.

Inconsistent claimant questionnaires, unverified diagnoses that appear once in the record without supporting workup, and missing operative, pathology, or radiology reports referenced elsewhere in the file but never actually obtained all fall into the same category: information the firm believes it has, in some form, but has not actually verified. Records belonging to another patient — a real and recurring error at the volume mass tort intake operates — and chronological inconsistencies within a single claimant's file round out the list of integrity failures this pillar is built to catch.

The purpose of a record integrity review is not simply to produce a longer list of outstanding record requests, though it does that as a byproduct. Its real purpose is to prevent a specific and expensive failure mode: false confidence. A record set that looks complete, and is treated as complete, but is not, can support a conclusion — in either direction — that the actual, complete record would not support. A claimant who appears weak on an incomplete file may in fact be strong once missing records are obtained. A claimant who appears strong may collapse the moment a missing operative report surfaces in discovery. Record integrity review exists to make sure the firm knows which of those two situations it is in before the case, not the opposing expert, forces the answer.

In Practice: A composite hernia mesh claimant illustrates the point directly. The claimant underwent mesh implantation, developed chronic pain and infection, and eventually required revision surgery — a fact pattern that looks compelling on its face. But without the original operative report, the revision operative report, and the explant pathology, the firm cannot actually determine whether the complication traces to the device, to surgical technique, or to the claimant's own baseline risk factors, which in this case included diabetes, obesity, and a prior wound infection. Record integrity review is what identifies, before the firm invests further, that this claimant's file cannot yet answer the question the case ultimately depends on.

None of this happens in ideal conditions, either. Provider record requests routinely take weeks or months to fulfill, some providers have closed or merged since treating the claimant, and statute of limitations pressure can force a firm to file before every gap is closed. A mature record integrity process distinguishes between records that are merely slow to obtain and records whose absence genuinely prevents a reliable classification, and it prioritizes chasing the second category with real urgency while tracking the first without letting it block the claimant's progress through the rest of the pipeline. The goal is not a perfect file before any decision can be made — it is an honest, documented account of exactly how complete the file is at the point a decision has to be made.

Chapter 6 — Pillar Two: Baseline Profiling

A claimant's condition before the alleged exposure defines the universe of what was already true, what risks already existed, and what alternative explanations the eventual causation analysis will need to rule out or account for. Baseline profiling is the pillar that establishes that starting point, and it is one of the pillars most frequently shortchanged in high-volume review, because it requires looking backward through the record rather than forward toward the claimed injury.

A rigorous baseline profile examines relevant pre-existing conditions and prior symptoms, even ones that were never formally diagnosed. It reviews previous diagnoses that may bear on the current claim, whether directly related or simply informative about the claimant's overall health trajectory. It catalogs medication history, prior surgeries, and any genetic or familial risk factors documented in the record. It accounts for lifestyle-related risk factors and occupational exposures that could independently explain some or all of the claimed condition, along with any previous use of similar products that could complicate the exposure story. Age-related risk, functional status before the alleged injury, and prior imaging or laboratory findings complete the picture.

None of this is pursued to undermine the claimant. It is pursued because baseline defines what was medically possible before the alleged tortious event, and that single sentence carries enormous weight in mass tort litigation specifically. Every causation argument the firm eventually makes — that this exposure caused this injury — is implicitly also an argument that the injury was not already present, was not already trending in that direction, and was not more plausibly caused by something else already documented in the claimant's history. A firm that has not done the baseline work cannot make that argument with any real confidence, because it does not actually know what was true before the exposure occurred.

The pillar also serves a second, more immediate purpose: it is often where a claimant's real weaknesses first become visible. A claimant whose current condition was already substantially present, at a similar severity, before the alleged exposure period is a claimant whose case may need to be reclassified — not necessarily disqualified, but understood very differently — long before that same fact surfaces in defense discovery, where it will be presented far less charitably than it would be if the firm had identified and accounted for it first.

In Practice: A composite anticoagulant claimant — prescribed the medication and later hospitalized for a major gastrointestinal bleed — shows why this pillar cannot be skipped even on an apparently strong file. Baseline profiling surfaces prior gastrointestinal ulcers, chronic kidney disease, a history of anemia, and concurrent use of another medication that independently raises bleeding risk. None of that eliminates the claim. It does eliminate the simplest version of it — that the medication created the ulcer outright — and redirects the case toward a narrower, better-supported theory: that the medication and a monitoring gap substantially worsened a condition that was already there. Appendix H works through this claimant's full causation map.

A caution belongs here, because baseline profiling is also where an overcorrected review process can do real damage to a portfolio. A firm that treats any baseline risk factor as automatically disqualifying will screen out a meaningful share of genuinely viable claimants, since very few people arrive at a mass tort exposure with a perfectly clean prior health history. The pillar's purpose is not to find a reason to decline every claimant with a comorbidity; it is to understand precisely how much weight that comorbidity should carry in the specific causation analysis for that specific claimant. A well-run baseline profiling process should be identifying nuance, not applying a blanket disqualification rule dressed up as clinical rigor.

Chapter 7 — Pillar Three: Imaging Analysis

Imaging deserves treatment as its own analytical pillar rather than as an incidental part of the broader chronology, because imaging findings do work in mass tort litigation that narrative summary cannot replicate. A radiology report is objective evidence in a way that a claimant's self-reported symptom history is not, and the difference between a claim supported by imaging and a claim supported only by subjective complaint is frequently the difference between a claim the defense can meaningfully contest and one it cannot.

Imaging can confirm or contradict an alleged injury outright, and it can establish whether pathology visible on a scan predates the exposure period, which folds directly back into the baseline analysis from the prior chapter. It can demonstrate whether a condition has progressed or remained stable over time, which speaks directly to causation and to damages. It can identify degenerative or clearly unrelated findings that a treating physician's narrative may not have distinguished from the claimed injury. It can reveal discrepancies between what a claimant has reported clinically and what the objective imaging actually shows — discrepancies that, left unaddressed, become a defense's opening argument. Imaging can support the claimed severity of an injury, establish anatomical plausibility for the mechanism alleged, and identify studies or reports referenced in the record but never actually obtained, feeding back into record integrity review. And because imaging findings can be genuinely ambiguous, this pillar also determines when further expert radiological interpretation is warranted, instead of leaving that judgment to a non-radiologist's read of a report summary.

The practical stakes are significant across the range of injuries mass tort litigation typically involves: product-related orthopedic injury, pulmonary disease, neurological injury, cancer progression, device migration or failure, organ damage, and vascular complications all depend, to varying degrees, on imaging evidence that a chronology-level review will note exists but will rarely interrogate closely enough to know what it actually shows. A structured imaging analysis pillar exists precisely to close that gap — not by replacing a radiologist's expertise, but by ensuring that every claimant's imaging has actually been examined for what it demonstrates, rather than simply logged as a document that exists in the file.

In Practice: A composite hip implant claimant demonstrates why the sequence of imaging matters more than any single image. Serial imaging shows progressive component loosening, tissue reaction consistent with wear debris, and no comparable findings on the unaffected side — a pattern a single scan could never establish on its own, and one that a claimant with a baseline history of obesity and prior hip trauma might otherwise struggle to distinguish from ordinary musculoskeletal pain. Appendix I walks through this claimant's full imaging analysis.

Imaging interpretation also carries a source of variability worth naming directly: two qualified radiologists reading the same study can reach genuinely different conclusions, particularly on borderline findings. A structured imaging analysis pillar should account for this rather than treating the first radiology report in the file as a final word. For claimants where imaging findings are central to the causation story and the initial read is ambiguous or contested, a second read — either from an in-house clinical reviewer trained to flag ambiguity or from a retained radiologist — is often the difference between a classification the firm can defend and one built on a single reader's judgment call.

Chapter 8 — Pillar Four: Timeline Reconstruction

Causation in mass tort litigation frequently turns on sequence and proximity: whether exposure, symptom onset, diagnosis, treatment, and outcome occurred in an order and at intervals that are medically plausible for the condition and exposure at issue. A well-constructed timeline is the tool that makes that question answerable, and it needs to be built from more than the handful of dates a chronology-level summary typically captures.

A complete timeline integrates the period, dose, duration, and frequency of product use or exposure; the point of first symptoms and initial clinical presentation; the diagnostic investigation that followed and the objective findings it produced; the treatment the claimant received; the documented progression of the disease or condition and any complications; the point of discontinuation of the product, where applicable; whether the claimant's condition improved or deteriorated afterward; any subsequent exposures that could complicate the causal story; and any later medical events that bear on either causation or damages.

Assembled with that level of completeness, a timeline does more than describe what happened — it establishes whether there was a medically plausible opportunity for the alleged exposure to produce the claimed outcome. That single question is often the fulcrum on which an entire claim turns. A claimant whose symptoms began well before meaningful exposure occurred, or whose diagnosis falls far outside any biologically reasonable latency period for the condition at issue, has a timeline problem that no amount of imaging or provider documentation can fully resolve. Conversely, a claimant whose timeline fits cleanly within the expected exposure-to-onset window, with no significant competing events, has a meaningfully stronger causation story than the same clinical facts would suggest in isolation.

Timeline reconstruction is also where many of the weaknesses identified in earlier pillars become visible as a pattern rather than as isolated facts. A gap in treatment noted during record integrity review, a pre-existing condition identified during baseline profiling, and an imaging finding from a date earlier than expected all take on their real significance only once they are placed on a single, complete timeline against the exposure period itself.

In Practice: A composite claimant alleging that long-term exposure to contaminated drinking water caused a kidney cancer diagnosis illustrates why latency, not just sequence, has to be built into the timeline. The claimant lived in the affected area for roughly fifteen years and was diagnosed several years after leaving. Establishing residence in a broad geographic area is not the same as establishing exposure to the specific water source, and simply confirming that exposure preceded diagnosis is not the same as confirming the interval is consistent with the disease's known latency. A timeline built to this pillar's standard has to integrate verified exposure duration, not just calendar sequence, before it can support a causation argument at all.

A related and easily underestimated problem is that timelines built substantially from claimant recollection are only as reliable as memory allows, and mass tort claimants are frequently being asked to date events — when symptoms first appeared, when a product was first used, when a particular provider visit occurred — that took place years or even decades earlier. Contemporaneous records almost always deserve more weight than a claimant's best current recollection, not because claimants are being untruthful, but because human memory reliably compresses, reorders, and reconstructs timelines under the pressure of trying to produce a coherent narrative. A timeline reconstruction pillar that defaults to the claimant's own account wherever a record is silent will tend to produce timelines that are cleaner, and more favorable, than the underlying facts actually support — which is exactly the kind of weakness a defense expert is trained to find.

Chapter 9 — Pillar Five: Standard of Care Review

5

Not every mass tort claim is limited to a straightforward product liability question. Many claimant files also involve provider, institutional, or treatment-related issues that sit alongside — and sometimes complicate — the core exposure-based claim, and this pillar exists to make sure those issues are identified rather than absorbed into the causation narrative without examination.

A standard of care review asks whether a claimant's symptoms were appropriately investigated when they first presented, and whether contraindications relevant to the exposure at issue were recognized by treating providers. It asks whether ongoing monitoring, where clinically indicated, was actually adequate, and whether providers responded appropriately to abnormal results rather than allowing them to go unaddressed. It examines whether relevant warnings were communicated to the claimant, whether treatment delays materially affected the outcome, and — critically — whether subsequent medical negligence, independent of the alleged exposure, interrupted or altered the causal chain the firm is trying to establish.

This pillar matters because it allows the firm to distinguish, with precision, between injury caused by the exposure itself and injury caused or worsened by independent, intervening medical care. That distinction is not a technicality. A claimant whose outcome was substantially worsened by a documented treatment delay or a missed abnormal result has a case that may still be viable, but one whose causation story — and whose damages calculation — needs to account honestly for that intervening factor rather than attribute the entire outcome to the original exposure. Firms that skip this analysis risk building a causation argument that a defense expert can partially dismantle simply by pointing to the claimant's own treatment record, in ways the firm should have identified and addressed first.

In Practice: The composite hernia mesh claimant introduced in Chapter 5 returns here for a different reason. Standard of care review asks whether the claimant's postoperative infection was recognized and treated promptly, and whether revision surgery was unreasonably delayed once warning signs appeared. Given a baseline history that includes diabetes, smoking, and a prior wound infection, this claimant was always at elevated risk for postoperative complications independent of the mesh itself. Whether the eventual outcome traces primarily to the device, to surgical technique, or to a delayed response to an infection that baseline risk made more likely in the first place is exactly the question this pillar exists to sort out — before the defense sorts it out first.

This pillar also has a practical limit worth naming: it is not a vehicle for turning every mass tort claimant into a separate medical malpractice case against their own treating providers, and it should not be applied that way. The purpose is narrower and more disciplined — identifying where intervening care affected the causal chain or the severity of the outcome, so the firm's damages theory and expert framing account for it honestly, not building a second cause of action the firm has no intention of pursuing. Reviewers applying this pillar need a clear standard for when a standard-of-care concern is significant enough to shape case strategy and when it is a minor documentation issue that does not meaningfully change the claim.

Chapter 10 — Pillar Six: Regulatory and Compliance Overlay

The same clinical facts can carry different legal significance depending on the regulatory environment in which the exposure occurred, and this pillar exists to make sure that context is applied deliberately rather than assumed. A firm that reviews the medical evidence in isolation, without overlaying the relevant regulatory history, risks either overstating or understating a claim's strength based on facts that were true at one point in time but not another.

Depending on the specific litigation, this overlay may draw on FDA warning and labeling history, adverse-event reporting data, product recall timelines, applicable Risk Evaluation and Mitigation Strategies, post-market surveillance findings, and manufacturer communications to providers or the public. It may involve contraindications and precautions in effect at the time of the claimant's exposure, device instructions, clinical monitoring requirements that applied to the product or condition, relevant institutional policies, and federal or state regulatory requirements and industry standards that governed the relevant period.

The chapter's central point is one that is easy to state and easy to underestimate in practice: warnings, labeling, and regulatory guidance change over time, and a claimant exposed before a particular warning was added is in a meaningfully different position than a claimant exposed after it. A causation and liability analysis that does not account for exactly when the claimant's exposure fell relative to that regulatory timeline is incomplete in a way that will matter enormously once the case reaches discovery, expert reports, or trial. Applying the regulatory and compliance overlay early — as part of the standard review process rather than as a late-stage discovery exercise — ensures every claimant's file reflects the regulatory reality that actually applied to them.

In Practice: For the composite anticoagulant claimant, the regulatory overlay means comparing the medication's label, bleeding-risk warnings, and monitoring recommendations as they existed during this specific claimant's eight-month treatment period against what the prescriber actually did — including whether continued prescribing despite declining hemoglobin was consistent with the guidance in effect at the time. The same clinical facts read very differently depending on which version of the label applied, which is exactly why this overlay has to be tied to the claimant's actual exposure dates rather than assumed from current labeling.

Applying this pillar consistently across a large portfolio requires building and maintaining what amounts to a regulatory timeline for the product or exposure at issue — every labeling change, safety communication, and recall date, organized chronologically, so that any claimant's exposure period can be checked against it directly rather than requiring a fresh regulatory research exercise for every file. Firms handling a single mass tort litigation typically build this timeline once, early, and then apply it as a standing reference across the entire inventory. Firms handling multiple concurrent litigations need a version of this reference maintained separately for each one, since applying one litigation's regulatory timeline to a different product's claimants is a mistake that undermines the credibility of the entire overlay.

Chapter 11 — Pillar Seven: Causation Mapping

Causation mapping is the pillar where the work of the previous six comes together, and it is the central analytical chapter in this section for a simple reason: nothing else in a mass tort claimant's file matters to the litigation if the causation story does not hold up.

A complete causation map draws on the exposure evidence and its dose and duration, the temporal relationship established through timeline reconstruction, the biological plausibility of the proposed mechanism, and the objective injury evidence surfaced through imaging and record review. It weighs baseline risk against alternative and contributing causes, accounts for any intervening events identified during standard of care review, and considers dechallenge evidence — whether the claimant's condition improved after discontinuing the product — and rechallenge evidence where applicable. It incorporates the available scientific and epidemiological support for the exposure-injury relationship generally, and then applies all of that to the claimant specifically: their individual strengths, their individual vulnerabilities, and the arguments a defense expert is most likely to raise against this particular file.

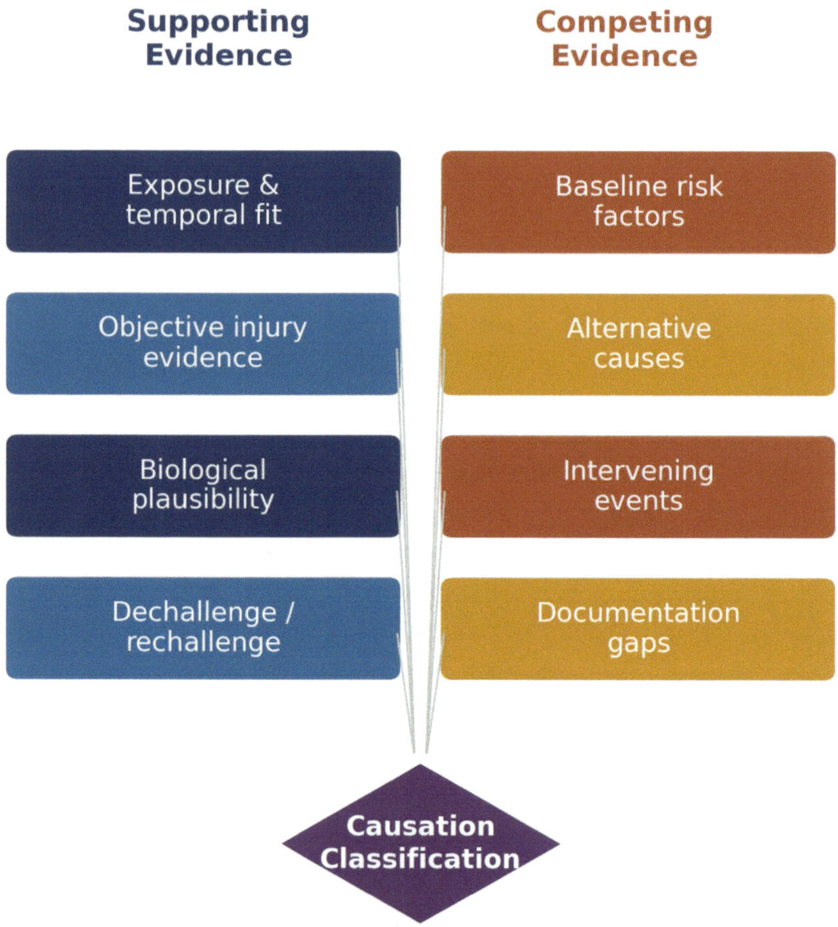

Figure 11.1 — Causation mapping weighs supporting evidence against competing evidence to reach a claimant-specific classification.

This pillar also requires precision in language that a general medical summary rarely provides. Causation mapping distinguishes between general causation — whether the exposure can cause this type of injury at all — and specific causation, whether it did so in this particular claimant. It distinguishes primary cause from contributing cause, aggravation from acceleration of a pre-existing condition, and genuine causation from coincidental association or evidence that is simply insufficient to support a conclusion either way.

That last category deserves particular emphasis, because the objective of causation mapping is not to force every claimant into a positive causation conclusion. It is to determine, honestly and rigorously, what the evidence can reasonably support. A model that only ever produces favorable conclusions is not a clinical intelligence model — it is an advocacy exercise wearing clinical language, and it will not survive contact with a well-prepared defense. The credibility of the entire methodology, and of every conclusion it produces about the portfolio's strongest cases, depends on its willingness to reach the same rigorous conclusion about the portfolio's weakest ones.

In Practice: The composite contaminated-water claimant is a useful illustration of the general-versus-specific causation distinction this chapter insists on. Scientific literature may well support general causation — that this contaminant is associated with this type of kidney cancer at sufficient exposure levels. That finding says nothing on its own about specific causation for this claimant, who also carries a significant smoking history, obesity, hypertension, a family history of kidney cancer, and prior occupational solvent exposure. Causation mapping keeps those two questions separate rather than letting a strong general-causation literature paper over a genuinely uncertain specific-causation picture for this particular claimant.

Because causation conclusions will vary in how confidently they can be stated, a mature causation mapping process documents not just the conclusion but the confidence behind it — distinguishing a claimant whose causation story is well supported and largely uncontested from one whose causation story is plausible but rests on a closer call the firm has made in the claimant's favor. That distinction matters enormously downstream: a firm negotiating settlement, selecting bellwethers, or briefing a litigation funder needs to know not just how many claimants fall into each causation category, but how much confidence sits behind each classification, so it is not treating a well-supported claim and a defensible-but-contestable one as equivalent simply because both were classified as causation-positive.

Chapter 12 — Litigation-Ready Output

Clinical Intelligence only creates value when it produces something an attorney can actually use, and this chapter closes Part II by describing how the seven pillars are converted from analysis into action.

The output of a completed Clinical Intelligence review should support claimant qualification decisions at intake, a defensible case-strength classification the firm can compare across its portfolio, a specific list of missing-record requests generated directly from the record integrity pillar, and an attorney case brief that translates the clinical findings into litigation terms rather than leaving that translation to the reading attorney. It should produce a causation summary grounded in the causation mapping pillar, a defense-vulnerability assessment that states plainly what an opposing expert is likely to argue, and a clear recommendation on whether and when expert referral is warranted.

The format of that output matters as much as its content, particularly at portfolio scale. A litigation-ready output that varies in structure from claimant to claimant — one reviewer's narrative organized one way, another's organized differently — forces every attorney who reads it to relearn how to find the information they need each time, which slows exactly the kind of rapid, comparative decision-making a large portfolio requires. A standardized template, applied consistently across every claimant regardless of who performed the underlying review, lets an attorney open any file in the inventory and know precisely where to find the causation summary, the defense vulnerabilities, and the recommended next step, without having to read the entire document to locate them.

At the portfolio level, this same output feeds bellwether recommendations, settlement support, deposition preparation, and trial strategy — each of which is the subject of its own chapter later in this book. What matters at this stage is the underlying principle: a Clinical Intelligence review that stops at analysis, without producing a structured, litigation-ready output, has not actually finished the job. The seven pillars are the discipline. The litigation-ready output is the product that discipline exists to create, and it is what allows a firm to move from understanding a single claimant's file to managing an entire portfolio with the same clarity — which is the subject of Part III.

PART III

III

Applying the Model Across a Portfolio

From individual case analysis to large-scale portfolio management.

Chapter 13 — The Mass Tort Clinical Intelligence Pipeline

Everything in Part II describes how to analyze a single claimant's file with clinical rigor. This chapter describes how that analysis is organized into a pipeline capable of moving thousands of claimants through the same disciplined process without collapsing under its own volume.

The proposed pipeline moves in a fixed sequence: claimant intake, record collection and validation, structured data extraction, record integrity review, baseline, imaging, and timeline analysis, regulatory and causation review, claimant classification, and finally an escalation or disposition decision that routes the claimant into the appropriate attorney, expert, settlement, or trial workflow.

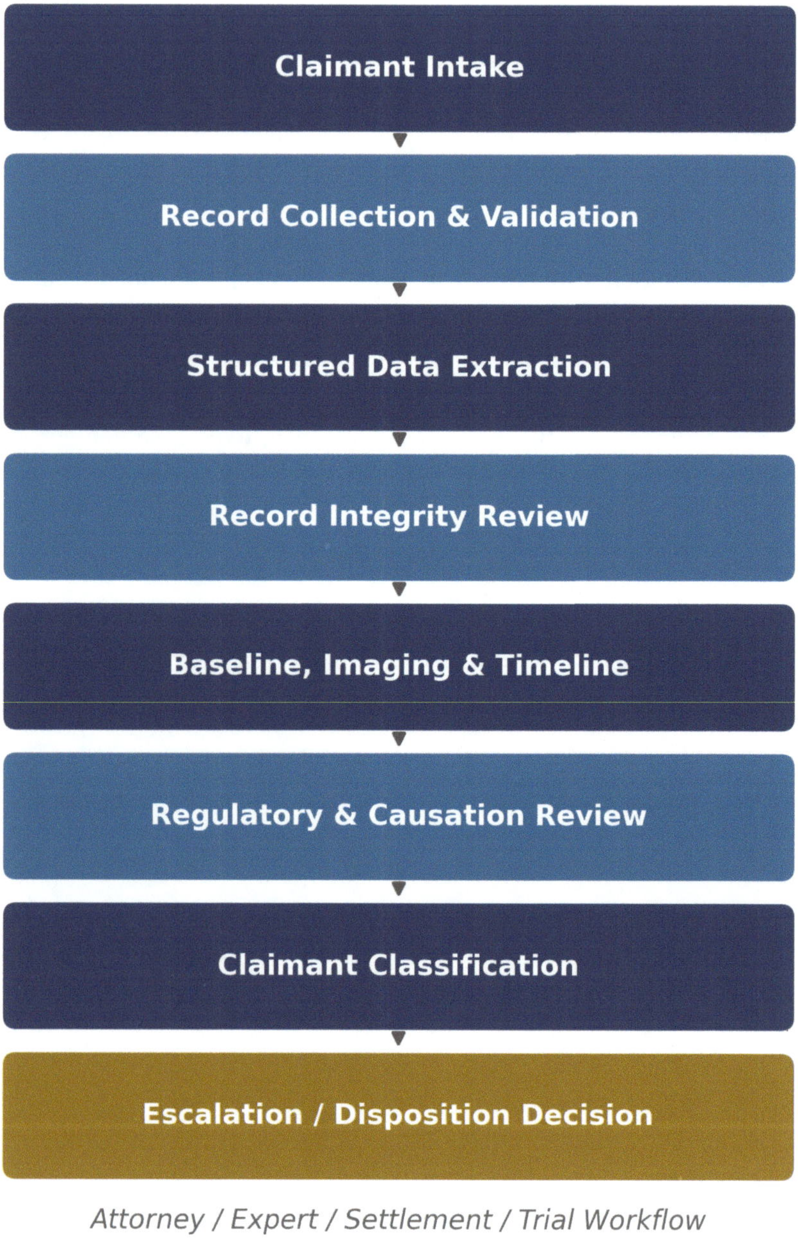

Figure 13.1 — The Mass Tort Clinical Intelligence Pipeline, from claimant intake through disposition.

The detail that matters most in this sequence is not any individual stage — it is the principle that different claimants move through the pipeline at different depths. A pipeline that applies the same expensive, senior-level review to every claimant at every stage has not actually solved the scale problem described in Chapter 1; it has simply relabeled it. The pipeline described in this chapter, by contrast, is built so that cases can be resolved — qualified, disqualified, or escalated — at the earliest stage the evidence allows, reserving the most expensive review capacity for the claimants who genuinely require it. That principle is the subject of the next two chapters: how early qualification narrows the inventory before expensive review begins, and how tiered review allocates the review capacity that remains.

A pipeline described this cleanly on paper still needs a clear answer to a question firms often leave unresolved: who owns it. A pipeline that spans intake, records, clinical review, and attorney-facing output cuts across departments that, in many firms, do not otherwise coordinate closely, and a pipeline without a single accountable owner tends to develop inconsistent handoffs at exactly the boundaries between those departments. The pipeline also cannot be treated as a one-way sequence. New records surface after a claimant has already been classified, imaging gets reinterpreted, a treating provider's deposition changes the standard-of-care picture — and the pipeline needs a defined mechanism for feeding that new information back into a claimant's existing classification rather than treating the original classification as permanent simply because the file has already moved further down the pipeline.

Chapter 14 — Intake Intelligence and Early Claimant Qualification

The earliest point in the pipeline is also the point where Clinical Intelligence has the most leverage, because a decision made at intake affects every dollar the firm spends on that claimant afterward. This chapter examines how the model improves claimant decisions before substantial capital has been committed.

Early qualification should establish minimum eligibility criteria specific to the tort at issue, verify exposure to the degree the intake record allows, and verify that an injury consistent with the litigation is actually documented rather than merely alleged. It should account for statute of limitations and timing considerations, and apply a preliminary alternative-cause screen — a first pass at whether an obvious, well-documented competing explanation already appears in the limited records available at intake. It should establish required-document thresholds below which a claimant cannot yet be meaningfully assessed, identify disqualifying factors that are already apparent, flag claims that need further investigation before a decision either way, and identify the claims whose intake documentation is already strong enough to justify immediate escalation to deeper review.

The emphasis throughout this stage should fall on a distinction that is easy to state and easy to lose in practice: identifying who appears eligible for the litigation is not the same as identifying who has sufficient clinical evidence to justify further investment. A firm that only screens for eligibility at intake, without also screening for evidentiary sufficiency, will fill its pipeline with claimants who technically qualify but whose files will not survive the deeper review still to come — at which point the firm has already spent the record-retrieval and administrative cost of onboarding them. Front-loading a genuine evidentiary screen, even a preliminary one, is one of the highest-leverage steps in the entire pipeline.

In Practice: The composite contaminated-water claimant is a clear illustration of why eligibility and evidentiary sufficiency are not the same question. Residence within the affected geographic area is enough to pass a minimum eligibility screen, and thousands of claimants in a given litigation may clear that bar. But residence in a broad area does not, by itself, verify use of the specific contaminated water source, at what concentration, or for how long — and a firm that treats geographic eligibility as equivalent to a strong claim will onboard a large share of claimants whose exposure evidence will not hold up once record integrity and timeline review actually test it.

Intake qualification is also frequently performed by the largest, least experienced review staff a firm has, simply because it operates at the highest volume — which makes calibration across reviewers essential in a way it is not at later, more senior review tiers. Two intake reviewers applying the same written criteria can still reach different eligibility decisions on similar files if they have not been calibrated against each other through shared examples and periodic cross-checks. Firms that skip this calibration step often do not discover the inconsistency until much later, when a portfolio-level audit reveals that claimants with materially similar intake profiles were qualified by one reviewer and declined by another, with no documented basis for the difference.

Chapter 15 — Tiered Clinical Review

Not every claimant who passes intake qualification requires the same depth of review, and a firm that treats them as though they do is simply moving the scale problem downstream rather than solving it. This chapter describes a tiered structure that matches review depth to what each claimant's file actually requires.

Level 1 is automated and administrative validation: confirming that required records are present, that claimant identity is confirmed, that exposure documentation has been identified, that basic injury criteria appear in the file, and flagging duplicate or incomplete records for correction before any clinical review begins.

Level 2 is Clinical Intelligence screening, applying a first pass of the seven pillars — baseline risk, imaging findings, timeline plausibility, initial causation indicators, material conflicts within the record, and any evidence still missing — sufficient to classify most claimants without requiring a full, senior-level review.

Level 3 is advanced clinical review, reserved for claimants whose Level 2 screening surfaced complex causation questions, multiple competing causes, significant comorbidities, unusually high-value injuries, genuine bellwether potential, or specific defense vulnerabilities that warrant closer examination before the firm decides how to proceed.

Level 4 is expert escalation: specialist interpretation, a formal causation opinion, an expert report, and deposition or trial support, reserved for the subset of claimants whose Level 3 review confirms that outside expert judgment is actually required, rather than sending every complex-looking file to an expert before the firm's own review has narrowed the actual question that needs answering.

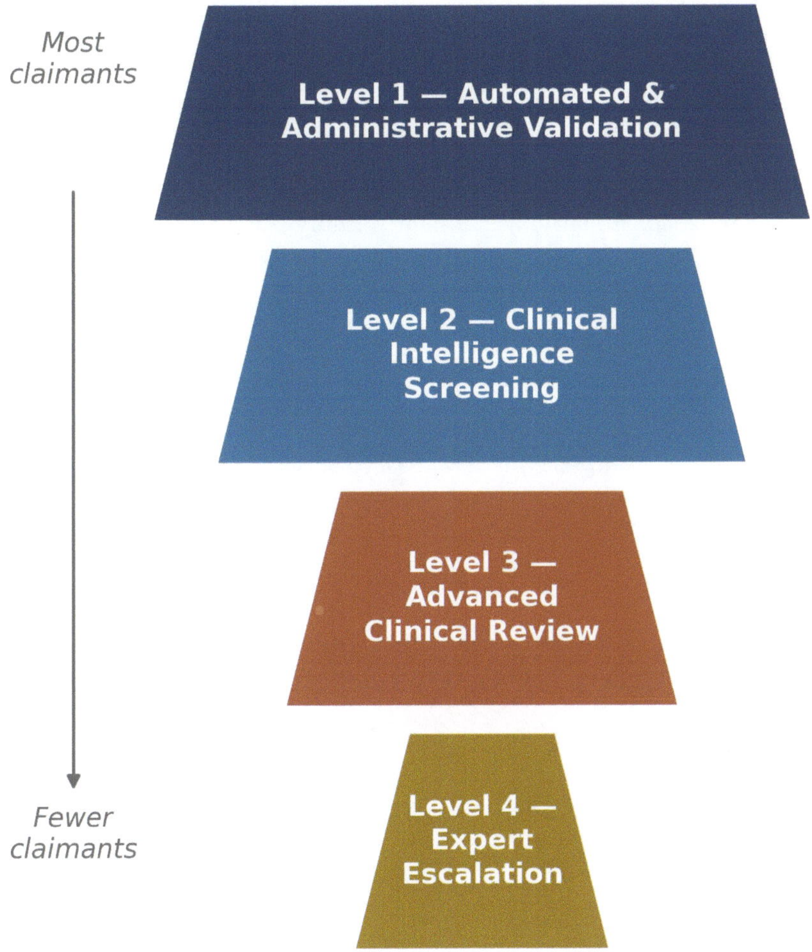

Figure 15.1 — Tiered review: review depth and cost increase from Level 1 to Level 4, while claimant volume decreases.

The economic logic of this structure is straightforward but easy to underestimate: most claimants can be reliably classified at Level 1 or Level 2, a smaller number genuinely require Level 3, and only a fraction of the total inventory ever needs to reach Level 4. A firm without tiered review effectively pushes far more of its inventory toward the most expensive levels than the evidence actually requires, because it has no earlier stage capable of resolving simpler cases on its own.

Tiers should also be understood as assignments that can move in both directions, not a one-time gate a claimant passes through once. A claimant classified at Level 2 based on the initial record set can move to Level 3 the moment newly obtained records surface a complication the earlier review could not have seen. Equally, a claimant initially escalated to Level 3 on a preliminary concern can sometimes be resolved back down to Level 2 once a specific missing record arrives and closes the open question cleanly. A tiered structure that only allows movement upward, treating every escalation as permanent, will over time push the entire portfolio toward the most expensive levels regardless of how the underlying evidence actually develops — which defeats the economic purpose the tiers exist to serve.

Chapter 16 — Claimant Classification and Portfolio Segmentation

Tiered review produces findings about individual claimants. Classification is what turns those findings into a structure the firm can actually manage a portfolio with — but this chapter opens with a caution that should govern everything in it: a classification is a support for professional judgment, not a replacement for it, and this book should be read that way throughout.

A workable classification framework might sort claimants into five priority categories: Priority A, strong clinical support across the pillars that matter most to the tort at issue; Priority B, supportive evidence that would benefit from specific additional records or investigation; Priority C, mixed clinical evidence where reasonable reviewers could differ on the claim's ultimate strength; Priority D, claimants with significant causation or documentation concerns that need to be resolved or accepted as a known weakness; and Priority E, claimants unlikely, on the evidence currently available, to justify further investment.

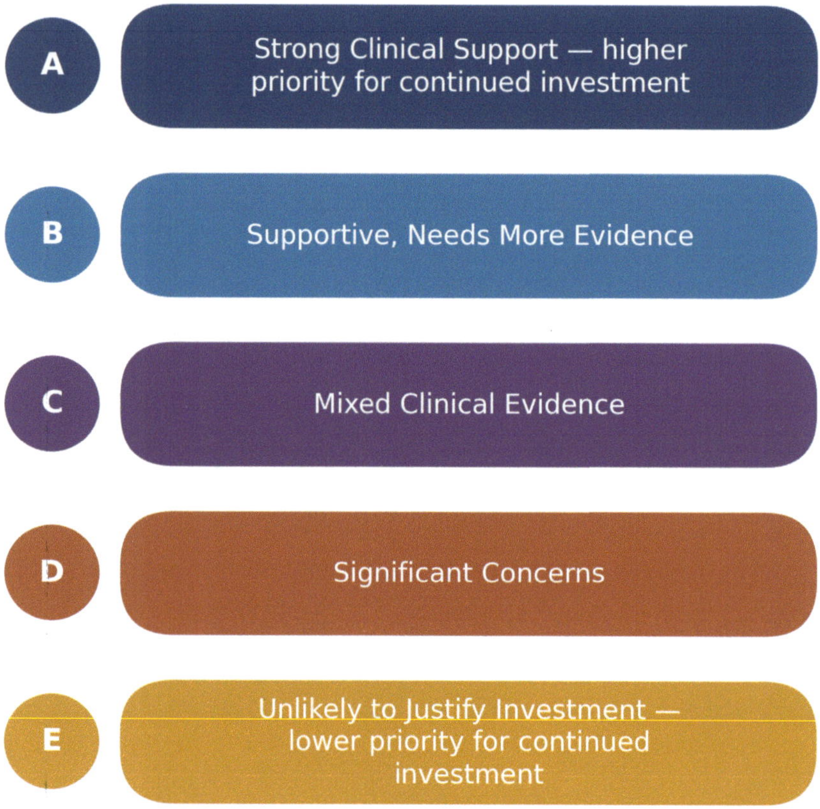

Figure 16.1 — The five-tier claimant classification spectrum, from strongest clinical support to lowest continued-investment priority.

The factors feeding that classification should be explicit rather than intuitive: exposure confidence, injury verification, record completeness, temporal strength, imaging support, baseline complexity, the burden created by plausible alternative causes, overall causation strength, identified defense vulnerabilities, and whether the claimant's file still requires expert-level review before its classification can be considered final.

The value of an explicit classification framework is not that it produces a single correct answer for every claimant — reasonable reviewers will still disagree at the margins, particularly for Priority C claimants. Its value is that it makes the firm's reasoning visible and comparable across the entire portfolio, so that priority decisions, resource allocation, and eventually settlement strategy can be defended with reference to a consistent standard rather than to whichever reviewer happened to touch a given file.

In Practice: A composite hair-relaxer claimant alleging that decades of product use contributed to a uterine cancer diagnosis shows why classification depends on more than a claimant's own account. A questionnaire response of "I used hair relaxers for years" is not, on its own, exposure evidence sufficient to classify a claimant as Priority A or B — it needs brand and formulation information, frequency, and ideally purchase or salon records behind it, weighed against baseline factors like obesity, diabetes, hormone exposure, and family history that also bear on uterine cancer risk. Two claimants with an identical diagnosis and an identical self-reported use history can land in very different priority tiers once the underlying exposure documentation and baseline profile are actually compared.

Classification systems are also vulnerable to a subtler risk that firms should build safeguards against directly: reviewer incentives that reward optimistic classification. A firm that measures individual reviewer performance primarily by how many claimants they push toward Priority A or B, or that creates any perception that declining a claimant reflects poorly on the reviewer, will tend to see classification drift upward over time regardless of what the underlying evidence actually supports. Periodic quality-assurance sampling — an independent second reviewer re-classifying a random subset of already-classified claimants and comparing results — is one of the more reliable ways to catch this drift before it distorts portfolio-level decisions built on the classification data.

Chapter 17 — Finding the Strong Cases Hidden in the Inventory

A large, unscreened inventory creates a specific and costly risk that is easy to overlook: genuinely exceptional cases get treated as routine ones, simply because nothing in the review process was designed to make them stand out. This chapter is about correcting that.

Clinical Intelligence, applied consistently across a portfolio, is specifically built to surface claimants with severe, objectively supported injuries; strong temporal relationships between exposure and onset; minimal alternative-cause burden; clear, well-documented exposure evidence; compelling before-and-after functional change; significant, well-supported economic damages; and strong demonstrative evidence more generally. These are the cases that deserve leadership attention, that may be well suited to bellwether consideration, and that can materially influence the trajectory of settlement negotiations for the entire portfolio if the firm recognizes them early enough to use them that way.

The risk this chapter addresses is not hypothetical. In an inventory of several thousand claimants processed through an undifferentiated review, exceptionally strong cases are statistically certain to exist, and equally certain to be missed for years if there is no structured mechanism to identify them ahead of the pack. A firm that only discovers its strongest claimants when they happen to reach an experienced attorney's desk, or when they are put forward for a bellwether pool built on incomplete information, has left significant leverage on the table for however long that discovery was delayed. Tiered review and explicit classification, applied consistently, are what make early discovery the rule rather than the exception.

In Practice: The composite hip implant claimant from Chapter 7 is a good illustration of a case that could easily sit unrecognized in a large inventory. On its face, it looks like any other implant complaint — pain, reduced mobility, a revision surgery. It is the serial imaging progression, the elevated metal-ion levels tracking with worsening findings, and the partial improvement after the device was removed that mark it as genuinely strong. None of that becomes visible without a reviewer, or a system, actually assembling the imaging sequence and the timeline together — which is precisely the kind of case a tiered, structured review is built to surface early rather than years into the litigation.

Beyond claimant-by-claimant review, a firm with structured classification data can go further and query the portfolio proactively for the specific combinations of factors that tend to define its strongest cases — for example, searching across every claimant for the combination of objectively confirmed imaging progression, a clean temporal fit, and minimal documented alternative-cause burden, rather than waiting for those cases to surface individually as reviewers work through the queue in intake order. This kind of portfolio-wide query is only possible once classification factors are captured consistently and in structured form across the inventory, which is itself one of the more concrete arguments for the standardized classification framework described in the previous chapter.

Chapter 18 — Identifying Weakness Before the Defense Does

The credibility of Clinical Intelligence as a methodology depends on this chapter as much as on any other in the book, because a model that only ever finds strength is not a clinical model — it is advocacy dressed in clinical language, and it will not hold up under scrutiny. This chapter is about the discipline of finding weakness first, deliberately and early, rather than leaving the defense to find it first.

A rigorous weakness review looks for pre-existing symptoms that predate the exposure period, alternative exposures that could independently explain the claimed condition, unrelated disease progression documented in the claimant's history, and inconsistencies between what the claimant has reported at different points. It looks for normal objective findings where the claim would predict abnormal ones, for latency periods that stretch plausibility or fall outside a biologically reasonable window, and for treatment noncompliance that could complicate both causation and damages. It looks for subsequent injuries that could confound the causal picture, for exposure evidence that is thinner than the claim assumes, for conflicting medical opinions within the claimant's own treatment history, and for damages claims that the records themselves do not fully support.

None of this exists to make the firm's own cases look worse than they are. It exists to prevent a much more expensive outcome: being surprised by a weakness late in the litigation that a careful early review would have identified, contextualized, and — where possible — addressed, rather than encountering it for the first time in a defense expert's report or a deposition transcript. A firm that knows its own weaknesses in advance can decide how to manage them. A firm that learns them from the defense has already lost the ability to choose.

In Practice: The composite contaminated-water claimant returns here as a reminder of how much alternative-cause burden a single file can carry. This claimant's history includes a significant smoking history, obesity, hypertension, and a family history of kidney cancer — any one of which a defense expert could point to as a sufficient independent explanation for the diagnosis. A firm that runs this weakness review early can decide, deliberately, whether to invest further in strengthening the exposure and latency evidence to outweigh that burden, or to classify the claimant accordingly and manage expectations — rather than discovering the same alternative-cause argument for the first time in the defense's expert report.

Firms adopting this discipline should also give early thought, with their own counsel, to how weakness findings are documented and where they are stored. Identifying a claimant's vulnerabilities early is unambiguously valuable for case strategy; how that identification is recorded, labeled, and routed within the firm's systems is a separate question with real discovery implications, and it is better addressed deliberately at the point a review process is being designed than reactively after a weakness-review document has already been created in a form the firm did not intend. This is not a reason to avoid finding weaknesses early — the alternative, letting the defense find them first, is worse in every respect discussed in this book. It is a reason to build the documentation practice thoughtfully rather than as an afterthought.

PART IV

IV

The Economics of Clinical Intelligence

Translating clinical rigor into cost, risk, and portfolio return.

Chapter 19 — The Economics of Case Acquisition

Every claimant a mass tort firm acquires creates a future financial obligation, whether or not that claimant's case ever produces a recovery. This chapter exists to make that obligation visible before it is incurred, rather than after, because the single highest-leverage economic decision in mass tort practice is not how a claim is eventually resolved — it is whether the claim should have been acquired, at the terms it was acquired, in the first place.

The full cost of a claimant runs well beyond the advertising spend that brought them to the firm's attention. It includes intake processing, record retrieval across every provider identified, record processing and organization once retrieved, the clinical review hours applied at whatever tier the file requires, attorney time spent on the file at every stage, expert consultation where warranted, filing fees, discovery costs, deposition preparation and execution, trial preparation for any claimant that proceeds that far, ongoing portfolio administration, the technology infrastructure that supports all of the above, and, for firms that finance their litigation costs, the financing costs attached to carrying the claim over what can be a multi-year timeline.

Laid out this way, the acquisition decision looks less like a single choice and more like the opening commitment in a long, compounding financial relationship between the firm and the claim. A firm that acquires claimants without a rigorous, clinically grounded view of their likely strength is not simply taking on legal risk — it is committing capital, on uncertain terms, to obligations that will recur at every subsequent stage of the litigation. Poor claimant selection does not merely fail to generate revenue in a neutral way; it compounds cost across the entire remaining life of the case, which is precisely the subject of the next chapter.

There is also a psychological dimension to acquisition economics that firms rarely name directly but that shapes real decisions: once a firm has already spent meaningfully on advertising and intake to bring a claimant into the pipeline, that spend creates pressure to proceed regardless of what a clinical review later finds, simply because declining the claimant means acknowledging the acquisition spend produced nothing. This is a sunk-cost dynamic, and it runs directly counter to good claimant selection. A firm's review process needs to be structured, and its incentives aligned, so that a clinical finding of weakness is treated as valuable information rather than as a loss to be avoided — because the acquisition cost is spent either way, and the only question left is whether the firm compounds it further or stops it here.

Chapter 20 — The Cost of Carrying Weak Claims

A weak claim sitting in a firm's inventory is not a cost-neutral placeholder waiting to be resolved. It is an active, ongoing drain on the firm's resources and attention, and this chapter is built around a principle that deserves to be stated as plainly as possible: the cost of a weak case is not limited to what the firm spends on that claimant directly. It includes the resources diverted from stronger cases that could have used them instead.

The direct costs are real enough on their own — continued record-retrieval expense as additional providers are identified, repeated staff review each time the file is touched for a status update or a discovery deadline, and, in the worst cases, unnecessary expert expenditure applied to a claimant whose weakness a more rigorous early review would have already identified. But the indirect costs are usually larger, and they are almost never tracked, because they are opportunity costs rather than line items: administrative burden that scales with inventory size regardless of claimant quality, reduced attorney attention available for the portfolio's stronger cases, portfolio projections distorted by claimants who will never actually resolve favorably, settlement negotiations complicated by an inventory the other side can credibly characterize as including a meaningful share of weak claims, increased discovery exposure created by files the firm has not fully investigated, and a general erosion of negotiating credibility that follows a firm known for carrying weak inventory rather than curating a strong one.

None of this is an argument for reflexively declining difficult cases. It is an argument for knowing, as early as the evidence allows, which claimants in the inventory are weak, and making a deliberate decision about how to manage them — investigate further, resolve quickly, or decline — rather than allowing them to remain in the pipeline by default, consuming resources indefinitely simply because no one made an active decision to do otherwise.

In Practice: The composite anticoagulant claimant from Chapter 6 illustrates a cost that is easy to miss: the cost of pursuing the wrong theory rather than the wrong claimant. This claimant is not weak — the file supports a real claim. But pursued on the theory that the medication created the ulcer outright, the firm would be litigating a theory the claimant's own pre-existing records substantially undermine, spending discovery and expert budget defending a position weaker than the one the evidence actually supports. Early causation mapping does not just separate strong claimants from weak ones; it can save a genuinely viable claimant from being carried under the wrong theory.

Knowing a claimant is weak and actually acting on that knowledge are different things, and firms often struggle with the second more than the first. Without a clear, pre-agreed process for what happens once a claimant is classified as weak — who has the authority to resolve, decline, or further investigate that claimant, and on what timeline — a Priority D or E classification can simply sit in the file without changing anything, and the firm ends up paying for the clinical review without capturing the cost savings that review was supposed to enable. Assigning that decision right explicitly, before the classification framework goes live, is what turns a weak-claim finding into an actual reduction in carrying cost rather than an accurate label on a claim the firm continues to carry anyway.

Chapter 21 — Allocating Clinical Resources According to Case Value

The tiered review structure introduced in Chapter 15 is, at its core, an economic tool as much as a clinical one: it exists to reserve the firm's most expensive resources for the claimants who actually justify them, rather than distributing that expense evenly across an inventory whose claimants do not have evenly distributed strength.

Applied well, this means routine validation stays at the lowest appropriate level instead of routinely escalating to clinical reviewers by default. Clinical reviewers focus their time on claimants whose files genuinely require professional interpretation, not on administrative gaps a structured intake process should have already caught. Senior reviewers are reserved for claimants with truly complex causation questions instead of being pulled into files a more junior review could have resolved. Physicians and other specialists see only the claimants whose issues require specialist judgment. And experts are retained only after the specific issues requiring their opinion have been clearly defined by the firm's own review — not as a first step taken because the firm has no other way to determine whether a claimant's causation story holds up.

The economic effect compounds across a large portfolio in a way that is easy to underestimate from any single claimant's file. A firm that reduces, even modestly, the share of its inventory that reaches its most expensive review tiers is not simply saving money on the claimants it screens out earlier — it is freeing senior reviewer and expert capacity to spend more time on the claimants who actually warrant it, which improves the quality of work on the firm's strongest cases at the same time it reduces total spend on its weakest ones.

This allocation logic also feeds directly into staffing and capacity planning, which most firms handle reactively rather than as a forecast. Once a firm has enough historical data on what share of its inventory typically resolves at each review level, it can forecast Level 2, 3, and 4 capacity needs against expected intake volume for the coming period, rather than hiring or contracting reactively each time a bottleneck appears at a particular tier. A firm that knows, from its own portfolio history, that roughly a fifth of new intake will eventually require Level 3 review can staff toward that expectation deliberately — which is a very different position than discovering the bottleneck only once a backlog has already formed.

Chapter 22 — Earlier Decisions, Lower Portfolio Cost

Nearly every cost described in this section shares a common driver: how early the firm's decisions about a claimant are made, relative to how long that claimant has already been in the pipeline. This chapter makes that relationship explicit, because it is the single clearest argument for adopting Clinical Intelligence at intake rather than treating it as a late-stage litigation tool.

Earlier case acceptance or rejection decisions mean the firm spends fewer resources on claimants who were never going to be viable. Faster identification of missing records means fewer years pass before a decisive piece of evidence is finally obtained. Reduced duplicate review, achieved through a documented and shared analytical record instead of repeated ad hoc examination, saves staff time across the life of every claimant in the portfolio. Earlier expert escalation, applied only where truly warranted, gets the firm's most complex questions in front of the right specialist sooner. Earlier recognition of fatal weaknesses prevents the firm from continuing to invest in claims that were never going to resolve favorably. Faster identification of high-value cases lets the firm direct attention toward its strongest claimants while there is still time for that attention to matter strategically, instead of after settlement terms are largely set.

Beyond the claimant level, earlier and more accurate Clinical Intelligence findings support more accurate portfolio-level decisions: reserve and investment planning grounded in real classification data rather than optimistic assumptions, more accurate workload forecasting for review and legal staff, and more informed allocation of litigation funding across a portfolio whose relative strengths and weaknesses the firm actually understands. Every one of these benefits depends on the same underlying fact — that Clinical Intelligence findings arrived early enough to still change a decision, rather than merely documenting one that had already been made by default.

Firms that want to manage this deliberately can track a specific metric worth naming on its own: decision lag, the gap between the date a piece of decisive evidence entered the claimant's file and the date the firm actually acted on it. A short decision lag means the review process is functioning as intended — findings are reaching decision-makers while they can still change course. A long or growing decision lag, even on a portfolio with otherwise strong review metrics, is usually a sign that classification findings are being generated but not routed to whoever has the authority to act on them quickly, which quietly erodes most of the economic benefit the earlier chapters in this section describe.

Chapter 23 — The Return on Clinical Intelligence

It would be easy for this chapter to promise a specific return figure, and it would also be dishonest, because the actual return any given firm realizes depends heavily on its existing review process, its portfolio composition, and how rigorously it applies the methodology described in this book. What this chapter offers instead is a measurement framework a firm can use to calculate its own return, using its own numbers.

A firm applying this framework should track cost per claimant screened and cost per claimant ultimately qualified, since the gap between those two figures reflects exactly how much the firm is spending to filter its inventory down to viable claims. It should track the percentage of claimants requiring advanced, Level 3 or Level 4 review, since a well-functioning tiered structure should resolve a meaningful majority of claimants at earlier, less expensive levels. Record-completion time and the average number of review cycles per claimant both measure how efficiently the pipeline is actually operating, while expert-review utilization tracks whether expert time is being reserved for genuinely complex questions or absorbed by issues an earlier stage should have resolved. Time from intake to classification is a direct measure of how quickly the firm can act on what it learns.

Beyond process metrics, a firm should track outcomes: the number of weak cases identified and appropriately resolved before filing, the number of high-priority cases identified and escalated early enough to matter, the cost avoided through earlier disposition of claims that would not have succeeded, the settlement value achieved relative to each claimant's documented evidence strength, and, at the portfolio level, return on invested litigation capital.

A simplified way to frame the economic value created is as the sum of several distinct savings and gains: avoided expenditure on weak-case claimants, reduced duplicate work across the review pipeline, better allocation of expert resources toward claimants who genuinely require them, earlier identification of the portfolio's strongest cases, improved settlement preparation grounded in a defensible classification system, and reduced overall portfolio risk from fewer late-stage surprises. None of these figures should be presented, to firm leadership or to a litigation funder, as a guarantee of a particular verdict or settlement outcome. The honest and defensible claim is narrower, and ultimately more durable: Clinical Intelligence improves the quality, timing, consistency, and defensibility of the decisions a mass tort firm makes across its portfolio, and better decisions, sustained across thousands of claimants, produce measurably better economics even without any single case being guaranteed anything at all.

Firms adopting this framework should also set expectations honestly about its shape over time rather than only its eventual size. The first measurement period after implementation will often look worse on paper than the prior baseline, not because the methodology is failing but because the firm is now paying the upfront cost of structured review on claimants that, under the old process, would have been carried further before their weaknesses surfaced. The savings — avoided expert spend, earlier disposition of weak claims, better-prepared strong cases — accrue over the following periods as the earlier, more disciplined decisions work their way through the portfolio. A firm measuring return only against its first-quarter numbers risks concluding the methodology underperformed, when it is simply still early in a return curve that takes real time to materialize.

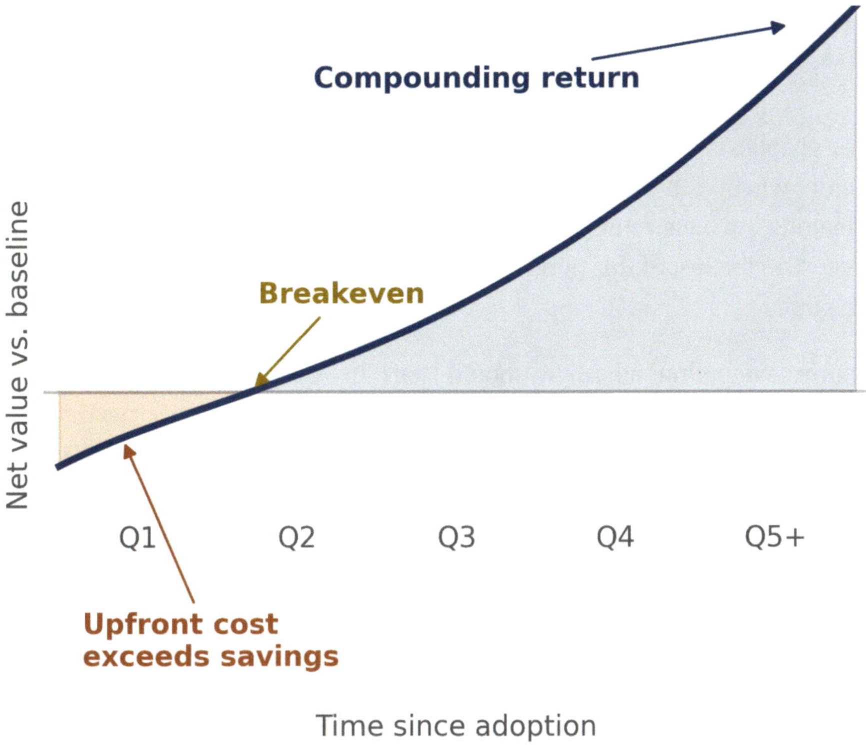

Figure 23.1 — The expected return shape: upfront review cost before breakeven, followed by compounding savings as earlier decisions work through the portfolio.

Chapter 24 — Building the Business Case for Enterprise Adoption

This chapter is written to be read on its own, by the audience most likely to decide whether a firm actually adopts Clinical Intelligence at scale — managing partners, chief financial officers, and litigation funders who may never read the rest of this book but who need enough here to make an informed decision.

A firm evaluating adoption should start by quantifying its own starting position: current portfolio size, average number of records per claimant, existing review costs, number of reviewers and their current workload, expert utilization rates, historical case attrition, typical review turnaround time, any known quality-control failures in the existing process, the litigation stage the portfolio is currently at, expected total portfolio duration, the anticipated cost of implementing a structured Clinical Intelligence process, the efficiency gains that process is expected to produce, and a reasoned estimate of the value created simply by reducing risk — fewer late-stage surprises, fewer weak claims carried unnecessarily, more defensible portfolio decisions.

A useful way to make the comparison concrete is to lay the two models side by side. Under the existing model common at many firms, every claimant receives broadly similar review regardless of complexity, the same work is frequently duplicated across different staff touching the same file, experts receive files that have not been clinically organized before reaching them, real weaknesses are typically discovered late — often during discovery or from a defense expert — and portfolio reporting is inconsistent because there is no shared standard behind it. Under the Clinical Intelligence model, claimants are triaged so review depth matches actual need, evidence gaps are identified early through structured record integrity review, experts receive focused, well-defined questions rather than an undifferentiated file, the portfolio's strongest cases receive earlier attention precisely when that attention has the most strategic value, and portfolio decisions are supported by a standardized, defensible classification system rather than by whichever reviewer happened to examine a given claimant.

Figure 24.1 — Existing model versus Clinical Intelligence model, side by side.

The business case, presented this way, does not ask a firm's leadership to take the methodology on faith. It asks them to compare a documented, familiar set of costs and risks under their current process against a structured alternative whose value can be measured using the same framework introduced in the previous chapter — cost per claimant, review-tier distribution, time to classification, and portfolio return — applied consistently from the moment the firm adopts it.

It is also worth presenting this decision to leadership as a phased investment rather than an all-or-nothing commitment, since framing it as the latter is one of the more common reasons a genuinely sound business case fails to get approved. A pilot on a defined, representative slice of the existing inventory — sized to be meaningful but small enough that the capital commitment and the risk of a flawed initial design are both contained — lets a firm test the methodology's actual performance against its own portfolio before committing to full deployment. The five-phase implementation roadmap in Part VI is built around exactly this logic, and firm leadership evaluating the business case in this chapter should understand that adoption does not require betting the full portfolio on the first attempt.

PART V

V

Litigation Strategy and Outcomes

Connecting the methodology to the moments that matter most in active litigation.

Chapter 25 — Clinical Intelligence and Bellwether Selection

Bellwether trials are meant to test the strength of a representative slice of the broader inventory, which makes bellwether selection one of the highest-stakes decisions in any mass tort litigation — and one that should not rest primarily on demographic representativeness or an individual attorney's instinct about which claimant will present well to a jury.

Clinical Intelligence brings a specific, evidence-based set of factors to that decision: exposure strength, injury verification, the clarity of the claimant's causation story, the burden created by any plausible alternative causes, credibility issues that are visible in the medical record itself rather than merely anecdotal, the degree of imaging and pathology support behind the claimed injury, the strength and clarity of the claimant's overall damages, how cleanly the medical narrative reads as a whole, identified defense vulnerabilities specific to that claimant, and how representative the claimant actually is of the broader group the bellwether is meant to inform.

The chapter's central warning is one every experienced mass tort attorney has likely seen play out: an apparently sympathetic claimant — someone whose personal story would resonate powerfully with a jury — can still have clinically weak evidence, and selecting that claimant as a bellwether risks a result that damages the entire portfolio's settlement leverage rather than strengthening it. Clinical Intelligence does not remove the value of a compelling personal narrative from bellwether selection; it ensures that narrative is paired with a clinical case strong enough to survive the scrutiny a bellwether trial specifically invites.

In Practice: The composite hip implant claimant discussed in Chapters 7 and 17 is the kind of file that tends to make a strong bellwether candidate — confirmed device identity, an objective imaging progression, elevated metal-ion levels, and, notably, partial improvement after revision surgery, which gives the claimant's causation story a persuasive before-and-after structure a jury can follow. That combination of objective evidence and narrative clarity is exactly what this chapter's factors are designed to identify before a firm commits to a bellwether pool.

Firms should also resist the temptation to build a bellwether slate entirely around their single strongest claimant. Concentrating bellwether risk in one file means the entire portfolio's settlement leverage rides on how one jury, one judge, and one set of case-specific circumstances happen to play out — and even a genuinely strong claimant can lose for reasons that have nothing to do with the underlying clinical merits. A slate built from several claimants who score well across this chapter's factors, but who vary in their specific injury profile, exposure circumstances, and demographic makeup, gives the litigation a more representative and more resilient test of the inventory, and it is a more defensible selection to present to co-counsel, a litigation funder, or the court overseeing bellwether selection in a coordinated proceeding.

Chapter 26 — Clinical Intelligence in Discovery

Discovery in mass tort litigation is where a firm's internal understanding of its claimants is tested against an adversary actively looking for gaps in that understanding, and a Clinical Intelligence review — completed well before discovery begins — changes how a firm approaches nearly every part of that process.

It allows the firm to prioritize discovery requests toward the evidence that will actually move a claimant's classification, instead of pursuing a generic, one-size-fits-all discovery plan across the whole portfolio. It identifies evidence still missing from the firm's own file, so that gap can be closed proactively instead of exploited by the defense. It supports preparation of plaintiff fact sheets grounded in a record the firm has already analyzed, not assembled at the last minute. It lets the firm test claimant consistency against the medical record before a deposition, instead of discovering an inconsistency during one. It helps the firm anticipate the specific defense medical arguments a given claimant's file is likely to invite, shape requests for production around the gaps the firm's own review has identified, and prepare treating-provider depositions with a clear sense of what testimony would strengthen or weaken the claim. It also identifies corporate or regulatory evidence — drawing on the regulatory overlay pillar from Chapter 10 — that bears directly on the clinical issues at stake for a given claimant or claimant group, and it supports building claimant-specific issue maps that keep the firm's discovery strategy organized around what matters to each file rather than a generic template.

This same specificity cuts in the firm's favor when it comes to proportionality, a principle defense counsel will invoke aggressively in any coordinated proceeding to limit the scope of what the firm can demand. A discovery request grounded in a documented, claimant-specific gap identified through record integrity review — "this specific pharmacy record is missing and directly bears on the dosage question in the causation map" — is far harder to characterize as a fishing expedition than a broad, templated request applied uniformly across the inventory. In multidistrict litigation specifically, where discovery strategy is typically coordinated through leadership counsel across many firms' claimants at once, having each firm's own claimant-specific gaps documented this clearly also makes it easier for leadership to build a common discovery plan that actually reflects what the collective inventory needs, rather than the lowest common denominator of what any one firm happened to request.

Chapter 27 — Expert Witness Strategy

An expert who receives a clinically organized case file, with the analytical groundwork already done, is in a fundamentally different position than one who receives an undifferentiated stack of records and is asked to form an opinion from scratch. This chapter addresses how Clinical Intelligence changes expert witness strategy specifically.

The methodology supports more precise expert specialty selection, since a completed causation map and imaging analysis will often make clear exactly what kind of specialist a given claimant's file actually requires. It allows the firm to frame focused referral questions rather than an open-ended request for a general opinion, which tends to produce sharper, more defensible expert reports. It ensures the expert receives a record the firm already knows is complete, or knows exactly where the gaps are, and flags conflicting evidence within the file before the expert encounters it unprepared. It supports the expert's own alternative-cause analysis by supplying the baseline and competing-cause work the firm's review has already done, identifies imaging issues worth the expert's specific attention, and can point toward relevant scientific literature the firm's own regulatory and causation review has already surfaced.

Beyond the initial opinion, this same groundwork supports deposition preparation — anticipating the questions opposing counsel is likely to ask based on the weaknesses the firm's own review already identified — and rebuttal strategy, since a firm that already understands its claimant's vulnerabilities is far better positioned to prepare its expert for how the defense will attack them. It also, quietly, prevents one of the more common and avoidable costs in mass tort litigation: retaining an expert to answer a question the firm's own Clinical Intelligence review could have already resolved, and paying expert-level rates for work that did not require expert-level judgment.

In Practice: For the composite hip implant claimant, a clinically organized file means the retained orthopedic expert receives the serial imaging already sequenced, the metal-ion trend already charted against the imaging timeline, and a specific referral question — whether the documented findings are more consistent with a device-related mechanism, a surgical malposition mechanism, or some combination of the two — rather than a general request to review the file and offer an opinion. That focused framing is what separates an expert report built to withstand cross-examination from one that simply restates the chronology.

Firms managing expert strategy across a large inventory also benefit from maintaining a standing roster of vetted experts organized by the specific specialty questions the litigation tends to raise, rather than sourcing an expert freshly for every claimant that reaches Level 4 escalation. A roster built this way lets the firm match a claimant to an already-vetted expert quickly, track that expert's prior opinions across similar claimants for consistency, and budget expert spend against expected Level 4 volume rather than treating each expert engagement as an unplanned expense. It also creates a useful internal check: if two claimants with materially similar causation profiles are producing meaningfully different expert conclusions, that discrepancy is worth investigating before either opinion is relied on further.

Chapter 28 — Settlement Intelligence

Everything this book has described at the individual claimant level eventually needs to scale into something usable at the settlement table, where a firm is negotiating not one claimant's outcome but the outcome for an entire portfolio or a defined settlement class within it. This chapter describes how claimant-level Clinical Intelligence becomes portfolio-level settlement intelligence.

A firm with a mature Clinical Intelligence process can support the development of settlement tiers grounded in real classification data rather than rough approximation, apply consistent injury classification across the negotiating group, and weight causation strength explicitly in how claimants are grouped and valued. It can identify exceptional cases that may warrant individual treatment outside a standard settlement matrix, and separately identify claimants who still need additional evidence before their value can be fairly assessed at all. It can evaluate proposed settlement criteria — whether from opposing counsel, a claims administrator, or a special master — against the firm's own classification data to judge whether those criteria are actually fair to the portfolio's real composition. It supports comparison of clinically similar claimant groups to check for consistency, prepares the firm for special-master or claims-administrator review with documentation already organized around the questions that process will ask, and supports individual claimant submissions with a clinical narrative that has already been through the discipline described in this book rather than assembled hastily at the point of submission.

A settlement matrix built early in the litigation should not be treated as fixed once it is built. As more claimants move through review, as bellwether outcomes provide real data on how juries respond to particular fact patterns, and as the defense's own positions become clearer through discovery, the matrix should be revisited and recalibrated against what the firm has actually learned. A matrix that was reasonable when built on a partially reviewed portfolio can become a poor fit for the fully reviewed inventory it is eventually applied to, and firms that treat their first settlement framework as permanent risk under-valuing claimants whose strength became clearer later, or overvaluing claimants whose early classification did not hold up under closer review.

The underlying argument of this chapter is one that should be familiar by now: a firm that enters settlement negotiations with a rigorously classified portfolio is negotiating from a position of genuine knowledge about what it holds. A firm that enters those same negotiations without that classification is negotiating on estimate, hope, and whatever the loudest voices in the room happen to believe about the portfolio's strength — a position that rarely serves claimants or the firm well.

Chapter 29 — Preparing for Defense Challenges

A Clinical Intelligence methodology that only ever produces conclusions favorable to the firm's own claimants would not survive serious scrutiny, and this chapter exists to make explicit that the model is built to test the claimant's case actively, not simply to advocate for it.

The defense issues this chapter anticipates are the same ones a well-prepared defense team will actually raise: alternative causation grounded in the claimant's own documented history, pre-existing disease that predates the exposure period, insufficient or absent proof of actual exposure, dose or duration too limited to plausibly cause the claimed injury, latency problems where the timeline does not fit what is biologically expected, diagnoses that are not well supported by objective findings, imaging that conflicts with the claimed injury, intervening events that complicate the causal chain, documented treatment noncompliance, injuries that occurred after the exposure period and may be unrelated, inconsistent or unsupported damages claims, and, in some torts, genuine scientific uncertainty about the underlying exposure-injury relationship itself.

Working through this list deliberately, for every claimant rather than only the ones that already look complicated, is what gives the methodology its credibility. A firm that can say, honestly, that it tested each of these questions against its own claimant files before the defense ever raised them is in a fundamentally stronger position — both because it has already resolved the issues it can resolve, and because it has not overstated the strength of claims that could not withstand that scrutiny.

Firms that want to pressure-test this further can build a structured adversarial review step into the process for higher-priority claimants: assigning a reviewer who did not perform the original classification to argue the defense's strongest position against the file, using the same list of issues this chapter provides, before the case ever reaches an actual defense expert. This is a deliberately uncomfortable exercise for whoever built the original classification, and that discomfort is exactly the point — a defense argument surfaced internally, by a colleague working from the same list a real defense expert will use, is a far cheaper and more manageable discovery than the same argument surfaced for the first time in opposing counsel's expert report. Findings from this exercise, especially defense arguments that prove more effective than expected, should also be fed back into the firm's standard review criteria so the same vulnerability is caught earlier across the rest of the portfolio, not just corrected for the one claimant where it happened to surface.

Chapter 30 — Litigation-Ready Clinical Narratives

An attorney working a mass tort portfolio does not need another lengthy medical summary that leaves the work of determining significance to the reader. This closing chapter of Part V describes the standard a litigation-ready clinical narrative should meet, translating everything in the seven pillars into a document an attorney can actually use under deadline pressure.

A narrative built to that standard states clearly what happened to the claimant, what the objective evidence demonstrates rather than merely what has been alleged, what existed before the exposure period, what changed afterward and precisely when it changed, whether that sequence is medically plausible given what is known about the exposure and the condition, what evidence supports causation, and — with equal directness — what evidence weakens it. It states plainly what evidence is still missing from the file, what a well-prepared defense is likely to argue given everything the record shows, and what action the legal team should consider taking next, given all of the above.

The right length and format for this narrative is not fixed — it depends on who is reading it and why. An attorney doing a quick portfolio-level triage across dozens of files needs a one-page summary that leads with the classification and the two or three facts that drive it. An attorney preparing for a deposition or drafting an expert referral needs the fuller narrative with complete supporting detail behind each conclusion. Producing both from the same underlying Clinical Intelligence review, rather than writing a single fixed-length document and hoping it serves every purpose, is worth the modest additional effort — and every version should carry a clear date and an indication of what records were considered as of that date, since a narrative written before a decisive record arrived is a different document, in every way that matters, from the same narrative written after.

That final element is what distinguishes a litigation-ready narrative from a medical summary, however well written. A summary describes. A litigation-ready narrative, produced through the discipline this book has described across its first thirty chapters, tells the attorney what the evidence means and what to do about it — which is, ultimately, the entire purpose of Clinical Intelligence as a discipline, and the bridge into the final section of this book, where that same discipline is scaled into an enterprise-wide operating system for the firm's entire portfolio.

PART VI

VI

Enterprise Clinical Intelligence

The operational infrastructure needed to apply the model at scale.

The Clinical Intelligence Command Center™

Everything in this book so far describes a methodology. This chapter describes the operational infrastructure that lets a firm actually run that methodology across a claimant inventory measured in the thousands, rather than applying it well to a handful of files and losing consistency as volume grows.

A Clinical Intelligence Command Center™ coordinates claimant intake, record ingestion, document classification, structured data extraction, clinical review queues organized by tier, specialty escalation when a claimant's file requires it, quality assurance checks, attorney reporting, expert referral, portfolio-level dashboards, audit trails, version control across every stage of review, and the security and access permissions that keep sensitive claimant data appropriately protected throughout.

It is worth being precise about what this infrastructure is, and is not. It is not simply a piece of software the firm purchases and deploys. It is the operational expression of everything described in Parts II and III — the seven pillars, the tiered review structure, the classification framework — made consistent, auditable, and repeatable across a claimant population too large for any one person to track manually. A firm can, in principle, apply the Clinical Intelligence Model without a Command Center, the way a smaller firm might apply it to a modest inventory using disciplined manual process. But as inventory scales into the thousands, the infrastructure stops being a convenience and becomes the only realistic way to keep the methodology from degrading into exactly the inconsistent, undifferentiated review process this book opened by describing.

Firms deciding how to build this infrastructure face a genuine build-versus-buy decision, and it is worth evaluating deliberately rather than defaulting to whichever option a firm happens to be more familiar with. Building in-house gives a firm complete control over the methodology's implementation and avoids dependence on a vendor's roadmap, but it requires sustained technical investment most firms are not otherwise staffed for. Adopting a commercial platform is faster to deploy and shifts much of that technical burden elsewhere, but it requires close scrutiny of whether the platform's underlying logic actually reflects the seven-pillar methodology this book describes, or merely automates the same shallow chronology-and-summary process Chapter 2 already identified as insufficient. The right evaluation question for any vendor is not how fast the platform can process a claimant file, but whether it can show its work at every one of the seven pillars, in a form the firm could defend to a funder or a court.

Human Judgment, AI, and Clinical Governance

Artificial intelligence has an obvious and growing role in a system built to process claimant records at scale, and this book takes a deliberately balanced position on what that role should be — because an unbalanced position, in either direction, undermines the credibility of everything else in this methodology.

AI can meaningfully assist with document classification, data extraction, date normalization, duplicate detection, generating an initial chronology from extracted records, identifying missing documents against an expected set, recognizing patterns across a large claimant population, and aggregating findings at the portfolio level in ways no human team could do manually at the same speed.

AI should not independently determine final causation, standard of care, claimant credibility, expert conclusions, legal merit, settlement value, or case disposition. Each of those determinations requires clinical and legal judgment that carries real consequences for real claimants, and delegating them to an automated system — however sophisticated — would abandon the exact discipline this book has spent thirty chapters building.

Operating responsibly at the boundary between those two categories requires specific governance controls: human clinical oversight over every conclusion that affects a claimant's classification or disposition, source citation so every AI-assisted finding can be traced back to the actual record it came from, full auditability of how a conclusion was reached, defined confidence thresholds below which a finding is routed to human review rather than accepted automatically, clear escalation rules, version control as records and analyses are updated over time, rigorous data security given the sensitivity of the information involved, formal model-governance standards, and an explicit prohibition on the system generating conclusions the underlying evidence does not actually support. AI, governed this way, becomes a force multiplier for the methodology. Ungoverned, it becomes exactly the kind of false confidence Chapter 5 warned against — just produced at much greater speed.

Firms relying on a third-party vendor for any of this AI-assisted functionality should extend the same governance expectations to that vendor rather than treating a vendor relationship as a reason to relax them. Reasonable questions to put directly to any vendor include what data the underlying models were trained on, how the vendor validates output accuracy against ground truth, what happens when the system's confidence in a finding is low, and whether the firm retains the ability to audit individual outputs down to their source records rather than receiving only an aggregated result. A vendor unable or unwilling to answer these questions clearly is not a vendor whose output should be relied on for claimant-level clinical determinations, however polished the platform's interface.

Standardization Without Losing Individual Case Meaning

Firms operating at mass tort scale need consistency across their claimant population, but every individual claimant remains, in fact, an individual person with a specific and particular medical history. This chapter addresses how to hold both of those truths at once, because a system that resolves the tension by sacrificing either one produces a worse outcome than the tension itself.

Standardization should apply to data fields, review criteria, required evidence thresholds, scoring and classification definitions, escalation rules, report structures, and quality-control checkpoints — the scaffolding that makes claimants comparable to one another and makes the firm's process defensible and auditable. What should never be standardized away is the individualized analysis underneath that scaffolding: each claimant's actual baseline condition, their specific exposure history, the particular character of their injury, their own timeline, the causation story specific to their file, their actual damages, and the defense vulnerabilities specific to their case rather than to the claimant population generally.

The test for whether a firm has struck this balance correctly is a simple one: a standardized process should make it easier to see what is genuinely distinctive about a difficult claimant's file, not harder. If the standardization is functioning as intended, an unusual case still stands out clearly against the consistent baseline the process has established. If it has gone too far — treating the framework as a substitute for judgment rather than a support for it — unusual cases start to disappear into the average, and the firm loses exactly the kind of case-specific insight that Chapter 17 argued is where much of a portfolio's real value is hiding.

Standardized criteria also need to change over time — as new records reveal patterns the original criteria did not anticipate, as regulatory understanding of a product evolves, or as bellwether outcomes provide real feedback on which factors actually predict litigation success. When that happens, firms need a deliberate versioning discipline rather than simply updating the criteria and moving forward. Every claimant's classification should be tied to the specific version of the framework used to produce it, so that a portfolio-wide comparison is not silently mixing claimants scored against different standards. When criteria change meaningfully, previously classified claimants should be flagged for re-review under the updated standard rather than left permanently classified under a framework the firm has since concluded was incomplete.

Quality Assurance and Defensible Review

A scalable Clinical Intelligence process is only as credible as its ability to show its own work. This chapter addresses the quality controls that make a firm's conclusions defensible — to its own leadership, to a litigation funder, and eventually, if it comes to that, to a court testing the reliability of the firm's process.

A defensible review structure documents reviewer qualifications for every tier of review, applies defined review levels consistently rather than allowing ad hoc departures from the standard process, uses mandatory checklists so no pillar is skipped under time pressure, has clear triggers for secondary review when a finding is borderline or high-stakes, links every finding directly back to its source in the record, tracks contradictions within a claimant's file rather than allowing them to be silently resolved by whichever reviewer happens to notice them, documents every escalation decision and the reasoning behind it, maintains version control as a claimant's file and analysis evolve, applies clear release requirements before a classification is treated as final, keeps full audit logs, has a defined correction procedure when an earlier finding turns out to be wrong, and maintains conflict-of-interest controls appropriate to the firm's structure.

None of this is bureaucratic overhead layered on top of the methodology. It is what allows the firm to answer, credibly, the question that will eventually be asked about every classification it has made: how do you know? A firm that can answer that question with a documented, auditable trail is in a fundamentally stronger position than one that can only answer it by pointing to a reviewer's general experience and asking that experience to be taken on faith.

Firms implementing quality assurance sampling need a clear answer to how much sampling is actually enough, since sampling every file defeats the efficiency purpose of tiered review and sampling too little fails to catch the drift Chapter 16 warned about. A reasonable starting approach combines two sampling strategies rather than relying on one alone: a fixed random percentage of all classified claimants, sufficient to detect systemic drift across the reviewer population as a whole, plus targeted review of every claimant that sits near a classification boundary — the Priority B versus C or C versus D line — where a reviewer's judgment call has the most influence on how the claimant is ultimately treated. Boundary claimants are disproportionately where inconsistency actually shows up, and a sampling plan that only draws randomly across the whole portfolio will systematically under-sample exactly the claimants most likely to reveal a problem.

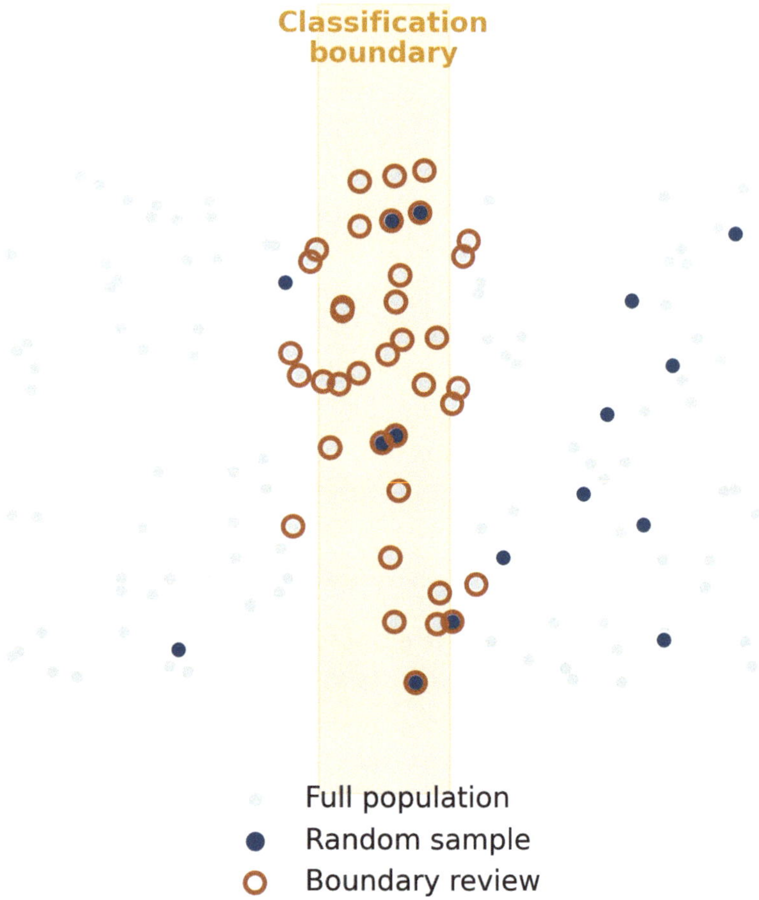

Figure 34.1 — QA sampling combines a random draw across the full population with targeted review of claimants near a classification boundary.

Implementing Clinical Intelligence in a Mass Tort Practice

This chapter closes Part VI with a practical roadmap for firms moving from reading about this methodology to actually adopting it, organized into five phases.

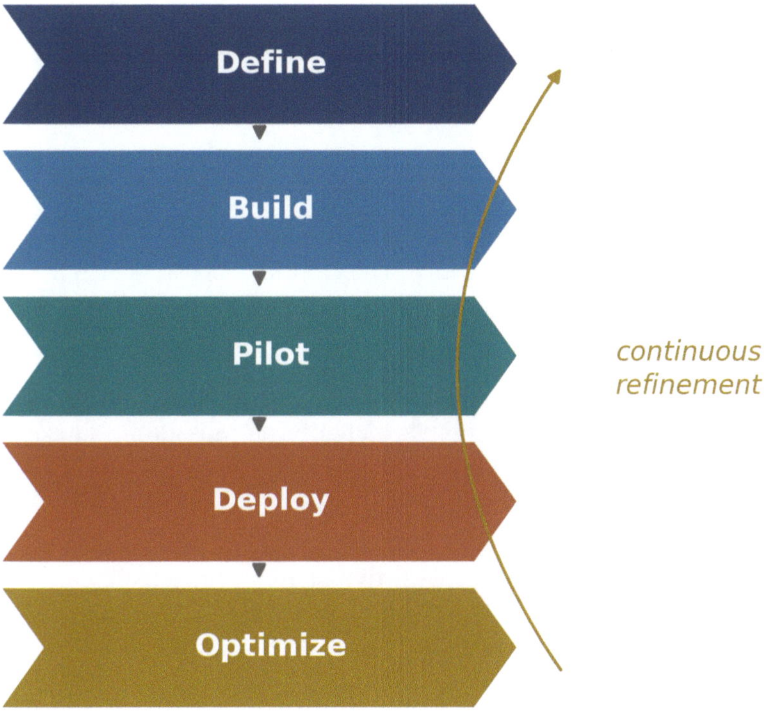

Figure 35.1 — The five-phase implementation roadmap: Define, Build, Pilot, Deploy, and continuous Optimize.

The Define phase establishes tort-specific injury criteria, exposure criteria, required records, known alternative causes relevant to the specific litigation, the applicable regulatory periods, and the key clinical questions the firm's review needs to answer for this particular tort. The Build phase turns those definitions into working infrastructure: intake logic, defined review pathways across the tiers described in Chapter 15, a classification framework calibrated to this tort, escalation rules, report templates, and quality-control checkpoints. The Pilot phase tests all of that against a genuinely representative sample of claimants, compares independent reviewers' conclusions against one another to check for consistency, measures actual turnaround time and cost against expectations, identifies where the process breaks down in practice rather than in theory, and refines the thresholds that govern escalation and classification before full deployment.

The Deploy phase trains reviewers on the finalized process, integrates the supporting systems, establishes the reporting firm leadership will actually use, begins full portfolio classification, and monitors quality as volume ramps toward the firm's real inventory size. The Optimize phase, which never really ends, analyzes outcomes against the framework introduced in Chapter 23, refines review pathways based on what that analysis shows, adjusts resource allocation across tiers as the portfolio's composition becomes clearer, updates the scientific and regulatory inputs that inform causation and compliance review as the underlying litigation evolves, and improves the firm's forecasting as more of its own portfolio data accumulates.

A firm does not need to complete all five phases before realizing value — a well-run pilot, on even a modest sample of claimants, is usually enough to demonstrate whether the methodology described in this book will work for a given firm's specific tort, portfolio, and existing process. What the five phases provide is a disciplined path from that first pilot to full enterprise adoption, without skipping the steps that make the difference between a methodology that works well on paper and one that actually holds up across a claimant inventory in the thousands.

A few failure modes recur often enough in pilot phases to be worth naming directly, so firms can watch for them deliberately. The most common is selecting a pilot sample that is not truly representative — often, unintentionally, a sample skewed toward the firm's strongest or most recently acquired claimants, which produces pilot results too favorable to predict how the methodology will perform against the full, more mixed inventory. A closely related failure is treating the pilot's timeline as fixed regardless of what it reveals, rushing through refinement to hit a planned deployment date instead of letting the pilot's findings genuinely shape the criteria before they are locked in. A third is failing to involve the attorneys who will use the litigation-ready output day to day in evaluating the pilot, so the methodology gets validated on clinical accuracy alone while the format and usability questions that determine whether attorneys adopt it in practice go untested until after full deployment, when they are far more expensive to fix.

PART VII

VII

The Future of Mass Tort Litigation

A closing argument for how firms should understand their own inventory.

From Case Inventory to Evidence Portfolio

The argument this concluding section makes is simple to state and, for many firms, difficult to fully act on: mass tort firms need to stop treating their claimant inventory as a list of names and start treating it as an evidence portfolio.

An evidence portfolio, understood this way, is not defined by how many claimants a firm represents. It is defined by claimant characteristics, exposure patterns, injury patterns, causation strength, evidence completeness, defense vulnerability, litigation readiness, economic investment already made, and strategic value across the group as a whole. Every methodology described in this book — the seven pillars, the tiered review structure, the classification framework, the economic measurement tools — exists to make that portfolio view possible in practice, not just as a conceptual reframe but as something a firm can actually see, measure, and act on across thousands of individual files.

That shift is ultimately cultural as much as it is technical. Tools and frameworks alone do not change how a firm behaves; leadership actually treating classification data as a real input to acquisition, staffing, and settlement decisions — rather than as a reporting exercise that runs alongside decisions made on other grounds — is what determines whether a firm becomes an evidence-portfolio firm in practice or simply adds a Clinical Intelligence label to the same decisions it was already making.

Clinical Intelligence as a Competitive Advantage

Firms that adopt this discipline should expect a specific and cumulative set of advantages over firms that continue managing mass tort inventory the traditional way. They should be able to make earlier decisions about which claimants to pursue and which to decline. They should understand their own inventory with a clarity most competitors do not have about theirs. They should protect litigation capital by directing it toward claimants who actually justify the investment. They should identify their most valuable cases earlier, prepare stronger experts by giving them clinically organized files rather than raw records, and negotiate settlements from a position grounded in real evidence rather than estimate. They should respond to defense challenges consistently, because the same rigorous methodology has already tested every claimant against the same questions a defense will eventually raise. They should be able to scale their inventory without abandoning the clinical rigor that made their early cases strong. And they should be able to demonstrate, to a funder, a co-counsel, or a court, a level of disciplined portfolio governance that a firm relying on undifferentiated review simply cannot match.

None of these advantages depend on having the largest inventory in a given litigation. They depend on understanding, with more precision and more consistency than anyone else in the room, what that inventory actually contains.

It is worth being honest, in closing this chapter, that none of these advantages appear overnight. As Chapter 23 described, the return on this discipline follows a curve, not a step change — the firms that benefit most are the ones that adopt it early enough, and stay with it consistently enough, for the advantage to actually compound across a full portfolio lifecycle rather than expecting it to resolve their next quarter's numbers.

Better Decisions Create Better Outcomes

This book has been careful throughout not to claim that the Lexcura Clinical Intelligence Model guarantees a particular verdict, a particular settlement figure, or any specific litigation outcome. That restraint has been deliberate, and it should extend to this final chapter as well.

What this book claims instead is narrower, and more durable: better outcomes begin with better decisions, and better decisions require a more complete understanding of the clinical evidence than most mass tort firms currently have access to at the scale their inventory demands. That is the entire premise the seven pillars, the tiered pipeline, the classification framework, and the economic measurement tools in this book were built to serve.

The closing principle is worth stating plainly, because it is the idea this entire book has been building toward from Chapter 1 onward: in mass tort litigation, the advantage does not belong to the firm that possesses the most records. It belongs to the firm that can determine — earlier, more consistently, and more accurately than anyone else — what those records actually mean.

PART VIII

VIII

From Clinical Finding to Litigation Decision

Translating completed Clinical Intelligence findings into the legal decisions attorneys must make.

Translating Clinical Intelligence Into Legal Issues

A Clinical Intelligence finding is not useful to an attorney until it has been translated into a legal question. This chapter makes that translation explicit, pillar by pillar, so that a reviewing attorney can move from a clinical statement to a litigation decision without having to make the connection themselves each time.

Missing diagnostic records

Attorney implication: qualification remains provisional; a targeted authorization or subpoena is required before the claimant's status can be finalized.

Weak exposure verification

Attorney implication: the product identification or exposure element of the claim may fail; further investigation is needed before the firm treats exposure as established.

Pre-existing disease

Attorney implication: the specific-causation theory must distinguish aggravation, acceleration, or contribution from the underlying condition, rather than assume the exposure is the sole cause.

Imaging predates exposure

Attorney implication: the claimed injury theory may need to be revised, since imaging evidence that predates the exposure period undercuts a straightforward causation story.

Strong dechallenge or improvement after removal

Attorney implication: this is potentially persuasive specific-causation evidence and should be flagged for early attention, expert framing, and possible bellwether consideration.

Latency inconsistency

Attorney implication: the expert theory, the pleading, or the firm's continued investment in the claim must be reconsidered in light of the timing problem.

Regulatory noncompliance

Attorney implication: depending on the governing law, this may support notice, defect, failure-to-warn, or impeachment analysis, and should be routed to the attorney responsible for that theory.

Alternative cause

Attorney implication: the alternative cause must be addressed — investigated, ruled out, or accounted for in the damages theory — before expert designation or deposition, not after.

Incomplete damages evidence

Attorney implication: settlement classification and any communication of claimant expectations should remain provisional until the damages record is complete.

This translation table is not exhaustive, and firms should expand it with findings specific to their own tort. What matters is the discipline it represents: every Clinical Intelligence finding should arrive at the attorney's desk already connected to the legal question it bears on, not as a clinical observation the attorney has to reinterpret from scratch.

In Practice: The pre-existing disease row is exactly the situation the composite anticoagulant claimant from Chapter 6 presented. Baseline profiling surfaced a prior ulcer and independent bleeding-risk factors well before the causation map was built, which meant the attorney handling that file never had to discover, mid-litigation, that the simplest version of the claim — that the medication created the ulcer outright — was vulnerable. The finding arrived already translated: the specific-causation theory needed to be aggravation, not creation, before the firm invested further in the wrong argument.

The Attorney Decision Matrix

Part III introduced the five-tier claimant classification — Priority A through E — as a clinical framework. This chapter attaches a mandatory attorney response to each tier. Without a defined response protocol, a firm can adopt the classification language and continue managing every claimant exactly as it did before, which defeats the purpose of building the classification in the first place.

Figure VIII.1 — The Attorney Decision Matrix: a mandatory response protocol attached to each classification tier.

Priority A — Strong Clinical Support

Attorney action: preserve the file, develop it further, route it to firm leadership for review, consider it for bellwether selection, and initiate early expert consultation while the evidence is freshest.

Priority B — Supportive, Needs More Evidence

Attorney action: continue the claim conditionally, obtain the specifically identified missing evidence, and set a firm reassessment deadline rather than leaving the claim open-ended.

Priority C — Mixed Clinical Evidence

Attorney action: assign the file for focused attorney review, work to resolve the competing clinical interpretations, and consider narrowly scoped expert input on the specific open question.

Priority D — Significant Concerns

Attorney action: determine whether the defect is curable, consider whether the legal theory needs to be repositioned, and limit further expenditure until that determination is made.

Priority E — Unlikely to Justify Investment

Attorney action: decline, withdraw, or administratively close the claim, retaining it only where a legal or contractual obligation independently requires continued action.

Each of these actions should be assigned to a specific responsible person and tracked against a deadline — Appendix M provides a template for doing exactly that across an entire portfolio. The point of the matrix is not to remove attorney judgment from the process. It is to make sure that judgment is actually exercised, consistently, every time a classification changes, rather than filed away and forgotten.

General and Specific Causation

This distinction is foundational to mass tort practice, and it deserves a direct, attorney-facing treatment rather than a passing mention.

Population-level evidence — epidemiology, mechanism studies, dose-response data — can establish that an exposure is capable of causing a type of injury, in general, across a population. This is general causation. It cannot, by itself, establish that the exposure caused this claimant's injury. That requires claimant-specific evidence: this person's baseline health, this person's exposure history, this person's latency period, this person's clinical progression, this person's diagnostic evidence, this person's treatment course, and this person's competing risk factors, weighed against each other for this individual.

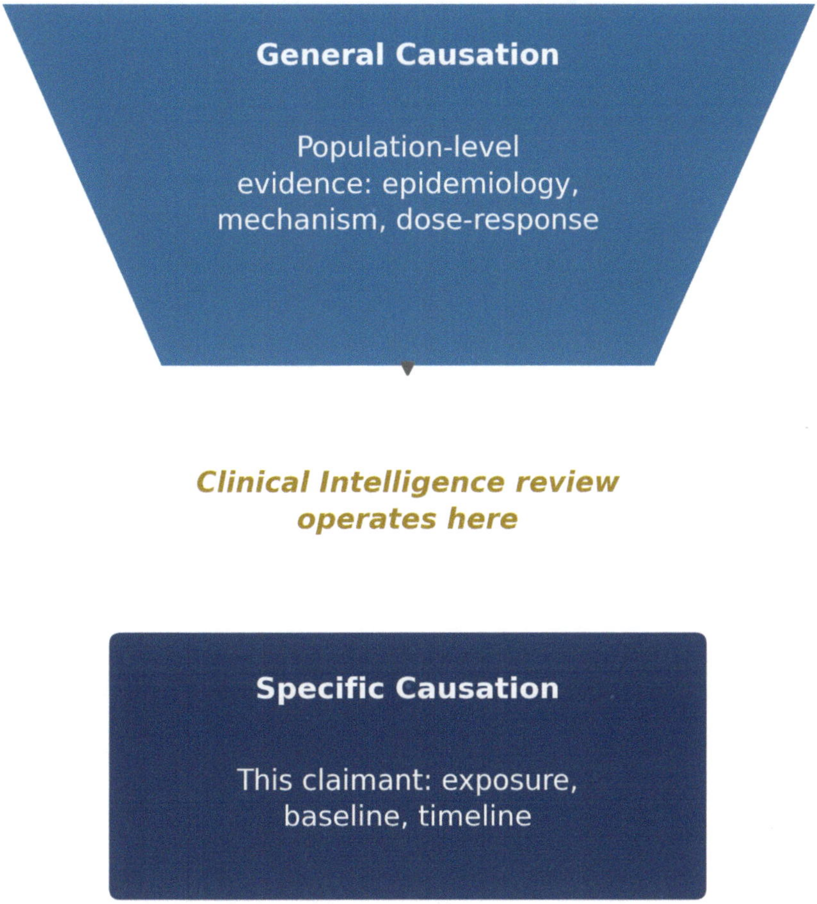

Figure VIII.2 — General causation narrows the population-level question; Clinical Intelligence review operates in the space between it and the claimant-specific answer.

A favorable general-causation ruling does not make every claimant in the portfolio viable. It clears a threshold question — that the exposure can cause this type of harm at all — and leaves the claimant-specific question entirely open. Conversely, a weak or contested general-causation environment limits what claimant-level Clinical Intelligence review can accomplish on its own, no matter how strong an individual claimant's specific evidence looks, because the underlying scientific proposition the claim depends on has not been established.

Clinical Intelligence review has a clear boundary here, and attorneys need to know exactly where it sits. The methodology in this book identifies, organizes, and weighs claimant-specific evidence — exposure, injury, timeline, baseline, competing causes — with rigor and consistency. It is not designed to establish general causation, and it is not a substitute for the retained expert analysis that formally connects a claimant's evidence to an admissible causation opinion. The reviewer's job is to prepare the claimant-specific record as completely and honestly as possible. The expert's job is to render the causation opinion the litigation actually requires. Confusing those two roles — treating an internal clinical screening as though it were expert testimony — is one of the more serious errors a firm can make, and this book does not endorse it at any point.

The practical reconciliation point is this: claimant-level Clinical Intelligence findings should inform the operative expert causation theory in the litigation, not compete with it or substitute for it. When a claimant's specific evidence does not fit the expert theory the litigation has adopted, that conflict needs to surface early — through the classification and escalation process described throughout this book — rather than being discovered for the first time when the expert actually reviews the file.

In Practice: The composite contaminated-water claimant illustrates why this distinction has real teeth. General causation in that litigation might be well supported — a genuine epidemiological association between the contaminant and this type of kidney cancer at sufficient exposure levels. That says nothing about whether this particular claimant, with a significant smoking history, obesity, hypertension, and a family history of kidney cancer, was actually harmed by the exposure rather than by one of several independent risk factors already in the record. A firm that treats a strong general-causation environment as settling the specific-causation question for every claimant in the geographic area is making exactly the error this chapter exists to prevent.

Evidence Admissibility and the Limits of Clinical Intelligence

This chapter is not a substitute for legal research or your own counsel's judgment on evidentiary questions, and it does not attempt to resolve jurisdiction-specific admissibility standards, which vary and change. Its purpose is narrower: to show attorneys where Clinical Intelligence's work ends and formal evidentiary proof begins, so the methodology is never mistaken for something it is not.

Federal Rule of Evidence 702, and the trilogy of Supreme Court cases interpreting it — *Daubert v. Merrell Dow Pharmaceuticals, Inc.*, 509 U.S. 579 (1993); *General Electric Co. v. Joiner*, 522 U.S. 136 (1997); and *Kumho Tire Co. v. Carmichael*, 526 U.S. 137 (1999) — generally require that expert testimony be based on sufficient facts or data, be the product of reliable principles and methods, and reflect a reliable application of those methods to the facts of the case. Rule 702 was amended effective December 1, 2023, and the amendment is worth knowing about specifically because it changes something courts had been getting wrong for two decades: it makes explicit that the proponent of expert testimony bears the burden of establishing admissibility by a preponderance of the evidence, and that a court must find not only that the expert's methodology is reliable in general, but that the expert reliably applied that methodology to this claimant's specific facts. Rule 703 separately addresses the facts or data an expert may reasonably rely on. Clinical Intelligence review can meaningfully support that process — by organizing the claimant-specific facts and data an expert will need, by identifying gaps before the expert encounters them, and by documenting the reasoning behind a claimant's classification — but the internal review itself is not expert testimony, is not independently admissible as causation proof, and should never be presented or relied upon as though it were.

Several distinctions are worth keeping firmly separate in how a firm talks about its own process: internal clinical screening, which supports case management decisions; consulting-expert analysis, which helps the firm understand a claimant's medical picture more deeply; testifying-expert opinion, which is formally disclosed and subject to challenge; and admissible causation testimony, which has survived that challenge and is available at trial. A firm's internal documents, review notes, and classification language should be written with this distinction in mind — describing what the record shows and what questions remain open, rather than using language that reads as a final legal or expert conclusion the internal reviewer was never positioned to reach.

Attorneys evaluating a claimant's causation posture should also keep in mind concepts that a testifying expert's own methodology will typically need to address: differential diagnosis or differential etiology reasoning; the fit between the expert's methodology and this specific claimant, not just the general theory; the distinction between objective and subjective evidence; the difference between temporal association and causal inference; where a proposed opinion sits within the medical literature hierarchy; the role of treating-physician testimony and learned treatises; and the limits of using regulatory action, on its own, as proof of causation. Clinical Intelligence review can flag where a claimant's file is strong or weak on each of these dimensions. It cannot resolve them — that is the expert's task, tested through the adversarial process the rules of evidence exist to structure.

In Practice: The composite hernia mesh claimant is a useful illustration of differential etiology specifically. That claimant's outcome could plausibly trace to a product defect, to surgical technique, or to baseline risk factors — diabetes, smoking, a prior wound infection — that independently elevate the risk of exactly the complications the claimant experienced. A testifying expert asked to opine on causation for this claimant will need a methodology capable of weighing these competing explanations against each other, not simply asserting the product-related pathway; the firm's own causation mapping in Chapter 11 is what tells the attorney, before the expert is ever retained, whether that weighing is likely to favor the claim or complicate it.

A Scientific Evidence Hierarchy

Firms building the source appendix described in Appendix L will inevitably need to weigh evidence of different kinds against each other, and it helps to have a shared, explicit hierarchy rather than an implicit, inconsistent one. Roughly in order of evidentiary weight for general-causation questions:

- Systematic reviews and meta-analyses
- Well-designed epidemiological studies
- Randomized or controlled evidence, where applicable to the exposure at issue
- Cohort and case-control studies
- Mechanistic and toxicological evidence
- Regulatory findings
- Case series and case reports
- Treating-provider opinion
- Claimant report
- Unsupported assumption

This hierarchy is a starting orientation, not a rigid formula — a single well-designed epidemiological study can outweigh several weaker case series, and mechanistic evidence can matter enormously when epidemiological data is still developing. What the hierarchy is for is preventing a specific and common error: treating a case report or a claimant's own account as though it carried the same evidentiary weight as a systematic review, simply because both are technically "evidence."

A few additional principles round out how this evidence should be read and recorded. The factors listed above — consistency, strength, temporality, dose-response relationship, biological plausibility, specificity, and replication across studies — are adapted from a subset of the nine criteria Sir Austin Bradford Hill proposed for judging causal inference from observed associations, in Hill, A.B., "The Environment and Disease: Association or Causation?", *Proceedings of the Royal Society of Medicine*, 58 (1965): 295–

300. Hill's original address included two further criteria — coherence with existing scientific understanding, and analogy to established causal relationships — that firms may also find useful depending on the exposure at issue; the framework has been the dominant reference point for causal reasoning in epidemiology and toxicology for six decades, and its terminology (particularly "biological plausibility" and "dose-response," sometimes called "biological gradient") will be familiar to any epidemiologist or toxicologist a firm retains as an expert. Firms should document which of these factors are present or absent for the general-causation proposition underlying their litigation. Absence of evidence is not the same as evidence of absence — a lack of published studies on a specific question does not itself establish that no relationship exists, and internal documents should not conflate the two. Conflicting scientific evidence should be recorded as conflicting, with both sides noted, rather than resolved silently in whichever direction is more favorable. And throughout, literature review of this kind informs the general-causation picture; it does not replace the claimant-specific analysis described in the rest of this book.

In Practice: The composite hair-relaxer claimant shows why this hierarchy matters practically, not just conceptually. A firm evaluating that litigation's general-causation posture needs to know whether the supporting evidence sits near the top of this hierarchy — a well-designed epidemiological study — or lower, resting more heavily on mechanistic plausibility and case reports. That placement shapes how confidently the firm can pursue the litigation at all, independent of any individual claimant's specific exposure history, and it is exactly the kind of firm-level judgment this hierarchy exists to support.

One Claimant, Start to Finish

Every pillar and every stage described in this book has, at some point, been illustrated through one of five composite claimants. This chapter follows a single one of them — the composite hip implant claimant introduced in Chapter 7 — through the complete arc: from initial questionnaire to final attorney decision. The purpose is to show how the pieces actually connect, not just how each one works in isolation.

1. Initial Claimant Questionnaire

The claimant reports a hip implant procedure roughly three years earlier, followed by what she describes as "ongoing pain that got worse." She recalls the implant brand approximately, is uncertain of the exact model, and reports a single revision surgery about a year before contacting the firm. She also reports, in general terms, that the pain affected her ability to work and to stay active with her family — the kind of functional detail that will matter later for damages, but that intake exists to capture, not to verify. Nothing in the intake conversation yet distinguishes this claimant from hundreds of others reporting similar symptoms, and the questionnaire itself should not be treated as evidence of anything beyond what the claimant recalls; Part VIII's guidance on distinguishing recollection from documentation applies from this first conversation onward.

2. Preliminary Qualification

The claimant clears minimum eligibility against the framework in Appendix B: an implant procedure within the relevant product's active-use period, a documented revision surgery, and no immediately apparent disqualifying factor. She is provisionally accepted into the inventory at Level 1 review. This is a gate, not a judgment on the claim's strength — it answers only whether the file is worth the cost of moving to the next stage, not whether the eventual claim will hold up. At this point the firm has spent intake time and minimal administrative cost; every subsequent stage increases that investment, which is exactly why the tiered structure exists.

3. Exposure Verification

Operative records confirm the implant procedure and, once obtained, the specific device identity — closing the uncertainty from the questionnaire. This single record converts an approximate, unverifiable claim of exposure into a documented one, and it is the record that everything downstream depends on: without confirmed device identity, imaging findings, regulatory overlay, and expert referral would all be built on an assumption rather than a fact. Firms handling claimants in volume should treat exposure verification as a genuine gate, not a formality — a meaningful share of claimants who pass initial questionnaire screening will not clear this step cleanly, and that attrition is the system working as intended, not a failure of intake.

4. Record Integrity Audit

The audit flags four gaps: the original implant lot information, complete operative records from the index surgery, serial radiology images, and the explant pathology report from the revision. A structured missing-evidence notice is generated automatically from this audit, tied directly to the discovery crosswalk in Appendix O so that each gap is already associated with the collection pathway most likely to close it — provider authorization for the operative and pathology records, and a direct request to the imaging facility for the radiology series.

Illustrative missing-evidence notice (excerpt): *"The following records are required before this claimant's file can be advanced beyond Level 2 review: (1) original operative report, index procedure; (2) explant pathology report, revision procedure; (3) serial radiographic imaging, index through revision. Requesting attorney: obtain via provider authorization; escalate to targeted subpoena if unproduced within 30 days."*

5. Baseline Profile

The claimant's baseline includes obesity, a prior hip trauma unrelated to the implant, and an abnormal gait pattern documented before the index procedure. None of these disqualify the claim, but each becomes a factor the eventual causation analysis has to address rather than ignore. Critically, baseline profiling happens here — before imaging and timeline review — precisely so that when the imaging findings arrive, the reviewer already knows what alternative explanations exist for hip-related symptoms in this specific claimant, rather than encountering the baseline risk factors for the first time after already forming a view of the case.

6. Imaging Review

Once obtained, serial imaging shows progressive component loosening over the eighteen months preceding the revision, tissue changes consistent with wear-related debris, and — critically — no comparable findings on the claimant's unaffected hip. That last point matters more than it might first appear: a claimant with the same baseline risk factors but bilateral, symmetric findings would tell a very different story, one pointing toward a systemic or baseline explanation rather than a device-specific one. The asymmetry here is doing real analytical work, not just adding color to the file.

7. Reconstructed Timeline

The timeline places initial post-surgical improvement, a gradual return of pain roughly ten months later, rising metal-ion levels tracking the worsening imaging, and, after revision, meaningful improvement — a dechallenge pattern the causation chapter identified as one of the more persuasive specific-causation signals available in a device case. Reconstructing this timeline required reconciling the claimant's own recollection (from step 1) against the actual dated records now on file, and where the two diverged — the claimant initially estimated the pain's return at "a few months," while the records place it closer to ten — the documented record controls, consistent with the guidance on claimant memory in earlier chapters.

8. Regulatory Overlay

The device's labeling and any relevant safety communications in effect during the claimant's implantation window are checked against what her treating surgeon's records show, establishing whether the applicable warnings and monitoring guidance were in place — and followed — at the time. In this claimant's case, the monitoring recommendations in effect during her treatment window called for periodic metal-ion testing following any reported increase in symptoms; the file is checked for whether that testing occurred at the point her symptoms began returning, which bears directly on the standard-of-care question as well as the product-related one.

9. General-Causation Assumptions Supplied by Counsel

Firm leadership designates the general-causation theory the litigation is proceeding under — that the device category is associated with an elevated revision rate tied to component wear. The claimant-level review proceeds against that assumption without attempting to independently establish it, consistent with the boundary drawn earlier in this Part: establishing general causation is counsel's and the retained experts' responsibility, not something the clinical review process is designed or positioned to do on its own.

10. Specific-Causation Analysis

Weighing the imaging progression, the dechallenge pattern, and the absence of comparable findings on the unaffected side against the claimant's baseline risk factors, the causation map (Appendix I) supports a device-related mechanism as the more likely explanation, with surgical malposition considered and not favored by the available imaging. The map does not conclude the alternative explanations are impossible — only that, on the evidence currently in the file, they are less well supported than the device-related theory. That distinction is preserved deliberately in how the finding is recorded, so that new evidence arriving later can update the analysis rather than contradict a conclusion that was overstated the first time.

11. Defense Vulnerability Analysis

An independent reviewer — someone who did not build the causation map in step 10 — is assigned to argue the strongest defense position the file currently supports, using the adversarial review discipline described in Chapter 29. The exercise is deliberately uncomfortable: it is designed to surface exactly what a well-prepared defense expert would raise, before that expert ever sees the file.

Illustrative defense-challenge extract: *"Claimant presents multiple independent risk factors for hip pain and early revision, including obesity,* *prior trauma, and pre-existing gait abnormality. Absent explant pathology, the mechanism of component wear cannot be confirmed. Claimant's own delay in reporting symptoms for approximately ten months post-surgery is inconsistent with device failure and more consistent with normal post-surgical recovery variability."*

Two of these three points are resolved by evidence already gathered by this stage — the reporting interval is explained by the reconstructed timeline in step 7, and the causation map in step 10 already accounts for the baseline risk factors. The pathology gap is real, unresolved, and exactly why this claimant's initial classification, in the next step, is provisional rather than final.

12. Initial Classification

On the record as it exists at this stage — before the missing operative and pathology records arrive — the claimant is classified Priority B: supportive, needs more evidence, with a defined reassessment deadline tied to the outstanding record requests. The classification is deliberately conservative given the still-open pathology gap identified in step 11; a firm that classified this file Priority A before the pathology confirmation arrived would be assigning a confidence level the record did not yet support.

13. Targeted Missing-Record Request

The firm issues the authorization and, when unproduced within the deadline, a targeted subpoena for the explant pathology report specifically, since that record is the single most consequential gap identified in step 4 and the one the defense-vulnerability analysis in step 11 identified as the file's central unresolved weakness. Prioritizing this one record over the other outstanding gaps is itself a judgment call, made explicit here rather than left implicit: not every missing record carries equal weight, and the discovery crosswalk in Appendix O is built to make that prioritization visible.

14. New Evidence Received

The explant pathology report arrives, confirming wear-related tissue changes consistent with the imaging findings and providing the objective confirmation the earlier classification was provisionally missing. This is the single piece of evidence the entire file has been waiting on since step 4, and its arrival is what moves the claimant from a provisional, evidence-pending status to a confirmed one.

15. Reclassification

With the pathology confirmation in hand, the claimant is reclassified Priority A: strong clinical support, under the version of the classification framework in effect at the time of reassessment, with the version and reassessment date logged per the discipline described in Chapter 34. The reclassification is recorded as a change from the prior Priority B status, not as a fresh classification — preserving the history matters, both for the firm's own audit trail and because a reviewer encountering this file later should be able to see exactly what changed and why, rather than only the current, final answer.

16. Expert Referral Decision

The file is referred to a retained orthopedic expert with a specific, pre-framed question — drawing directly on Chapter 27's guidance — rather than a general request to review the record: whether the documented findings are more consistent with a device-related mechanism, a surgical mechanism, or a combination, given the imaging sequence and the dechallenge pattern now on file. The expert receives the imaging already sequenced, the metal-ion trend already charted, and the defense-vulnerability analysis from step 11 already documented, so the referral is a focused second opinion on a well-organized file rather than a first pass through raw records.

17. Bellwether Assessment

Given the combination of confirmed device identity, objective imaging progression, and a persuasive dechallenge pattern, the claimant is flagged as a bellwether candidate under the factors described in Chapter 25, pending confirmation of representativeness against the broader claimant group. Being a strong claimant is necessary but not sufficient for bellwether selection — Chapter 25 also warns against concentrating an entire slate around a single claimant profile, so this flag routes the file into a broader bellwether-pool evaluation rather than an automatic selection.

18. Settlement Classification

The claimant's status is captured in a single-page format built for rapid review by anyone in the firm who needs it — a managing partner deciding where to focus attention, a funder asking for a portfolio snapshot, or another attorney picking up the file for the first time.

Illustrative one-page attorney dashboard (excerpt):

- Classification: Priority A (reclassified from Priority B)
- Exposure: Confirmed, specific device identity established
- Injury: Confirmed via imaging and explant pathology
- Causation: Device-related mechanism favored; surgical mechanism considered, not favored
- Key defense vulnerabilities: Baseline risk factors (obesity, prior trauma); reporting delay
- Outstanding items: None material
- Recommended action: Advance to bellwether consideration; retain expert referral response

19. Litigation-Ready Attorney Brief

Where the dashboard in step 18 is built for a five-second read, the case brief is built for the attorney who is about to prepare for deposition, negotiate a settlement tier, or brief co-counsel — someone who needs the reasoning behind the classification, not just the classification itself.

Illustrative attorney case brief (excerpt; see Appendix N for the full template): *"This claimant's file supports a device-related causation theory grounded in objective imaging progression and a favorable dechallenge pattern. Baseline risk factors are present but do not, on this record, provide a more persuasive alternative explanation than the documented mechanical findings. Primary litigation risk is the ten-month reporting delay, which should be addressed proactively in deposition preparation rather than left for the defense to raise first."*

20. Final Attorney Decision

The responsible attorney approves the claimant for continued development, bellwether consideration, and early expert consultation — the Priority A response protocol defined in this Part's Attorney Decision Matrix — closing the loop from an uncertain intake questionnaire to a fully developed, litigation-ready file. The decision itself is logged against the matrix in Appendix M, with a named responsible attorney and a reassessment date, so that even a fully developed Priority A file remains subject to the same discipline of review as every other claimant in the portfolio, rather than being treated as finished and set aside.

This is, deliberately, a favorable outcome. Not every claimant's file will resolve this cleanly, and Chapter 18's discipline of finding weakness first applies here as much as anywhere else. What this walkthrough is meant to show is not that every case ends at Priority A — it is how each stage in this book's methodology actually hands off to the next, and how a clinical finding, at every step, arrives at the attorney's desk already connected to a specific, actionable legal decision.

BACK MATTER

Appendices

Practical tools, designed to be used directly and adapted to your own tort, portfolio, and firm.

Appendix A — Mass Tort Clinical Intelligence Workflow

The full end-to-end workflow, from claimant intake through disposition into the appropriate downstream workflow, is shown below. See Chapter 13 for the discussion of how claimants move through this pipeline at different depths depending on what their file requires.

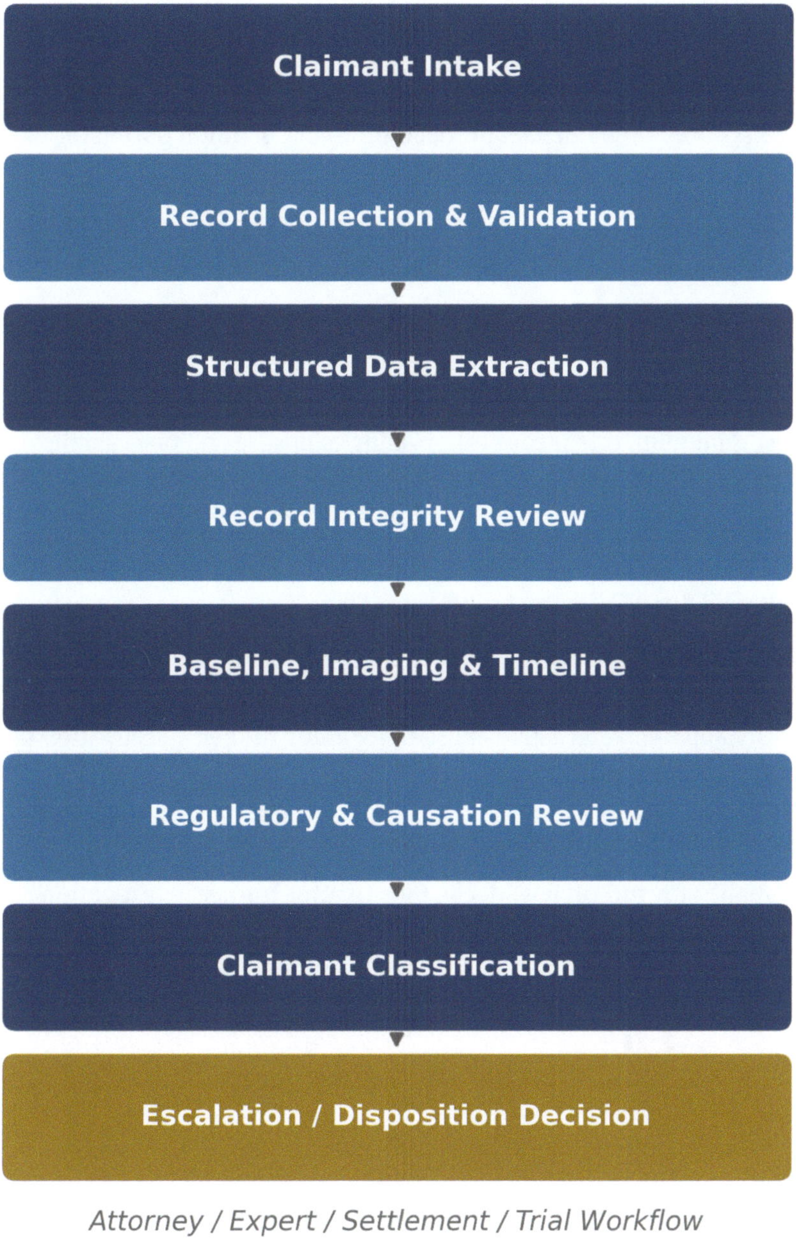

Figure A.1 — The Mass Tort Clinical Intelligence Workflow, end to end.

Appendix B — Claimant Qualification Framework

Minimum Eligibility Screen

- Exposure to the relevant product, drug, or condition during the applicable period
- Injury or diagnosis consistent with those recognized in the litigation
- Claim falls within the applicable statute of limitations
- Claimant identity and basic contact/records information confirmed

Documentation Threshold

- At minimum, one record establishing exposure and one establishing the injury are on file
- No unresolved duplicate or conflicting identity records

Preliminary Alternative-Cause Screen

- No single, obviously dominant alternative cause apparent from intake-level records
- Any apparent alternative cause flagged for further investigation rather than automatic disqualification

Disposition at This Stage

- Qualify for full review, decline, or flag for further investigation before a decision is made

Appendix C — Required Evidence Matrix

This matrix should be adapted to the specific tort at issue. As a starting structure, track the following categories for every claimant: exposure evidence (purchase, prescription, or occupational documentation), injury evidence (diagnosis, treatment records), baseline records (pre-exposure history), imaging, pharmacy records, pathology, operative reports, follow-up and ongoing treatment records, and damages documentation (lost wages, other economic impact). For each category, track whether the record is confirmed present, confirmed missing and requested, or not yet determined.

Appendix D — Seven-Pillar Review Checklist

Pillar One — Record Integrity

- All expected provider records obtained or formally requested
- No unresolved duplicate or conflicting documents
- No unexplained treatment gaps
- All referenced diagnostic studies and reports located

Pillar Two — Baseline Profiling

- Pre-existing conditions and prior symptoms documented
- Medication and surgical history reviewed
- Occupational and lifestyle risk factors reviewed
- Prior imaging and labs reviewed for baseline findings

Pillar Three — Imaging Analysis

- All relevant imaging identified and reviewed
- Findings compared against the claimed injury
- Discrepancies between imaging and clinical narrative flagged
- Need for expert radiological interpretation assessed

Pillar Four — Timeline Reconstruction

- Exposure period, dose, and duration documented
- Symptom onset and diagnosis dated and sequenced
- Timeline checked against known latency expectations
- Competing or subsequent events identified

Pillar Five — Standard of Care Review

- Investigation and monitoring of symptoms reviewed
- Provider response to abnormal findings reviewed
- Treatment delays or gaps assessed for impact
- Intervening negligence, if any, identified

Pillar Six — Regulatory and Compliance Overlay

- Applicable warnings, labeling, and recalls identified for the claimant's exposure period
- Relevant regulatory requirements for that period documented
- Changes in warnings over time accounted for

Pillar Seven — Causation Mapping

- General and specific causation addressed separately
- Alternative and contributing causes documented
- Dechallenge/rechallenge evidence reviewed where applicable
- Claimant-specific strengths and vulnerabilities stated plainly

Appendix E — Claimant Classification Framework

Priority A — Strong Clinical Support

Clear exposure, objectively supported injury, strong temporal fit, minimal alternative-cause burden.

Priority B — Supportive, Needs Additional Evidence

Generally favorable picture, contingent on specific missing records or further investigation.

Priority C — Mixed Clinical Evidence

Reasonable reviewers could differ; genuine strengths and genuine weaknesses both present.

Priority D — Significant Concerns

Meaningful causation or documentation problems that must be resolved, mitigated, or accepted as a known risk.

Priority E — Unlikely to Justify Further Investment

Evidence currently on file does not support continued investment absent a material change in the record.

Appendix F — Clinical Intelligence Economic Assessment Worksheet

Current-State Inputs

- Total current review expenditure (annualized)
- Expert utilization rate and average expert cost per claimant
- Average cost per claimant screened
- Estimated duplicate-review cost
- Estimated cost of delayed disposition on known weak claims

Projected Efficiency Gains

- Expected share of claimants resolved at Level 1 or Level 2 review
- Expected reduction in expert referrals reaching Level 4
- Expected reduction in duplicate review
- Expected reduction in time from intake to classification

Compare current-state spend against projected spend under a tiered Clinical Intelligence process to estimate net economic benefit before committing to full implementation.

Appendix G — Bellwether Clinical Assessment Framework

For each bellwether candidate, assess and document: exposure strength, injury verification and objective support, clarity of the causation story, alternative-cause burden, imaging and pathology support, damages clarity, identified defense vulnerabilities, and representativeness relative to the broader claimant group. Candidates with strong personal narratives but weak scores across these clinical factors should be flagged explicitly before any final selection decision.

Appendix H — Causation Mapping Example

The claimant is a composite, not an actual case: a 68-year-old prescribed a brand-name anticoagulant who suffered a major gastrointestinal hemorrhage eight months later, requiring hospitalization, transfusion, and intensive care. At first read, the file looks like a strong claim — confirmed medication use, a documented bleed, a transfusion, and lasting functional decline. Causation mapping is what determines whether that first read survives closer analysis.

Supporting Evidence

- Confirmed anticoagulant use beginning approximately eight months before the bleeding event
- Endoscopy-confirmed active gastric ulcer at the time of hemorrhage
- Worsening anemia documented after treatment began
- No record of a monitoring adjustment despite declining hemoglobin
- Continued prescribing after early warning signs were already present in the chart

Competing Evidence

- Prior gastrointestinal ulcers documented before the medication was ever prescribed
- Chronic kidney disease and a history of anemia independent of the medication
- Long-term concurrent use of an anti-inflammatory medication that independently increases bleeding risk
- Missing pre-exposure gastroenterology records, including a prior endoscopy report, that could clarify how active the ulcer already was

What the Map Shows

Baseline profiling establishes that the claimant did not begin this history free of ulcer disease — a pre-existing ulcer and an independent bleeding-risk profile were already present before the medication was prescribed. That single fact rules out the simplest version of the claim: that the medication caused the ulcer outright. It does not rule out a narrower and still meaningful theory. Timeline reconstruction shows worsening anemia and unaddressed warning signs after treatment began, and standard of care review identifies a monitoring gap and continued prescribing despite deteriorating labs. Together, those findings support a claim that the medication substantially increased the severity and duration of the bleed, and that delayed clinical response contributed to the outcome — aggravation of a pre-existing condition, rather than direct creation of the injury.

Classification and Litigation Value

This case illustrates why causation mapping resists a binary strong/weak answer. Pursued on the theory that the medication created the ulcer, this claim is vulnerable to a defense built almost entirely from the claimant's own prior records. Pursued on the theory that the medication and the monitoring gap substantially worsened a pre-existing condition, the same file supports a defensible, evidence-grounded claim. The value of the mapping exercise is not that it produces a favorable answer — it is that it identifies the correct question before the firm has spent discovery and expert budget on the wrong one.

Appendix I — Imaging Analysis Example

This composite claimant, 59 years old, received a hip implant and later developed persistent pain, reduced mobility, and elevated metal-ion levels, ultimately requiring revision surgery. The claimant also had obesity, prior hip trauma, an abnormal gait, and lumbar spine disease on record — any of which could independently explain some of the reported pain. Imaging is what separates a genuine device-failure claim from unrelated musculoskeletal symptoms in a claimant who was never going to be pain-free to begin with.

What the Imaging Sequence Shows

- Serial imaging demonstrates progressive component loosening over time, not a single static finding
- Changes are visible around the implant consistent with an ongoing process rather than a one-time event
- Imaging suggests possible malposition of the device
- Tissue reaction consistent with wear debris is present
- No comparable findings appear on the unaffected side, which weakens a purely degenerative or age-related explanation

Why the Sequence Matters More Than Any Single Image

A single image, viewed in isolation, might be explained away as an unremarkable finding in a claimant with this baseline profile. The progression across serial imaging is what does the real analytical work: it shows a mechanical process advancing over time in a way that a static degenerative condition would not produce, and it shows that process concentrated on the implanted side while the unaffected side remains unremarkable. Timeline reconstruction adds a second confirming data point — the claimant improved initially after surgery, then experienced a gradual recurrence of pain that tracked with rising metal-ion levels and worsening imaging findings, and then showed partial improvement again after the device was removed. Improvement after removal is one of the more persuasive causation signals available in a device case, and it only becomes visible when imaging and timeline are read together rather than separately.

Classification and Litigation Value

Because device identity and imaging progression are objective and well documented in this composite, and because the improvement-after-removal pattern is present, this claimant would likely classify as a strong candidate for advanced review — but only once the record integrity gaps common to implant cases are closed: the original device lot information, complete operative records, and the explant pathology report. Without those, even a compelling imaging sequence cannot be reliably tied to a specific device or confirmed mechanism of failure, and the case remains provisionally strong rather than litigation-ready.

Appendix J — Sample Portfolio Dashboard

A firm-level dashboard should track, at minimum: claimant status by pipeline stage, evidence completeness by claimant and by category, current review level for each open claimant, causation classification across the portfolio, outstanding missing records, escalation status, overall litigation readiness, and a summary view of portfolio risk concentration — for example, the share of the inventory currently classified Priority D or E.

Appendix K — Implementation Readiness Assessment

Before committing to full implementation, a firm should honestly assess: whether current portfolio size justifies the investment, whether existing review data is available to calibrate the pilot phase, whether staff are available to be trained across the review tiers, whether current technology infrastructure can support structured intake and review tracking, whether firm leadership is prepared to act on classification findings rather than treating them as advisory only, and whether the firm has a realistic timeline for moving through the five implementation phases described in Part VI without shortcutting the pilot stage. A firm that cannot answer most of these affirmatively is not necessarily a poor candidate for Clinical Intelligence — but it likely needs to address these gaps before, rather than during, full deployment.

Appendix L — Sources and Further Reference

This book draws on general, well-established principles of medical record review, litigation strategy, and mass tort practice rather than a single study or source. A small number of foundational, cross-tort authorities are cited directly below because they apply regardless of which mass tort a firm is litigating. Beyond those, the specific regulatory history, scientific literature, and case law relevant to any given mass tort differ substantially by product, exposure, and jurisdiction, so the remainder of this appendix is intentionally structured as a framework for your own team to populate rather than a fixed reading list — a generic tort-specific citation list would go stale the moment it was printed, and would not reflect the specific tort your firm is actually litigating.

Foundational References

These sources apply across mass tort practice generally and are cited directly because they are stable, verifiable, and not tort-specific.

- Federal Rules of Evidence 702 and 703, governing expert testimony and the facts or data an expert may rely on. Rule 702 was amended effective December 1, 2023.
- *Daubert v. Merrell Dow Pharmaceuticals, Inc.*, 509 U.S. 579 (1993); *General Electric Co. v. Joiner*, 522 U.S. 136 (1997); and *Kumho Tire Co. v. Carmichael*, 526 U.S. 137 (1999) — the trilogy of Supreme Court decisions establishing the modern framework for expert-testimony admissibility discussed in Part VIII.
- Hill, A.B., "The Environment and Disease: Association or Causation?", *Proceedings of the Royal Society of Medicine*, 58 (1965): 295–300 — the origin of the causation criteria referenced in Part VIII's evidence hierarchy chapter.

For each active or prospective litigation, consider building your own version of this appendix with:

- FDA labeling history, safety communications, and any recall documentation specific to the product or exposure at issue

- The general-causation scientific and epidemiological literature relied upon by both plaintiff and defense experts in the litigation, including any Daubert or admissibility rulings already issued in the MDL or coordinated proceeding
- Relevant treatises or practice guides on the specific tort category (pharmaceutical, device, environmental, or consumer product)
- Prior bellwether verdicts, settlement frameworks, or claims-administrator criteria from comparable litigations
- Internal firm resources: prior expert reports, deposition transcripts, and briefing that established precedent for how this exposure and injury combination has been argued before

Maintaining this appendix as a living document — updated as new science, regulatory action, or court rulings emerge — is itself an application of the Clinical Intelligence discipline this book describes: know what you know, know what has changed, and know what you still need to find out.

Appendix M — Attorney Action Matrix

A tracking template for applying the Attorney Decision Matrix (Part VIII) across an entire portfolio. For each claimant, record:

- Current classification (Priority A–E) and the framework version it was assigned under
- The specific clinical issue driving that classification
- The legal implication, using the translation table in Part VIII as a starting reference
- The responsible attorney or team member
- The deadline for the required action
- The next action itself, stated as a concrete task rather than a general instruction
- The reassessment date, tied to when new evidence is expected or when the deadline lapses

A firm can build this as a simple spreadsheet or as a view within its Command Center; what matters is that every claimant's classification has a corresponding row, and that no classification exists in the system without an assigned action and owner.

Appendix N — Sample Attorney Case Brief Template

A completed case brief should run two to four pages and cover, in this order:

Current Classification

State the priority tier and the date it was assigned.

Executive Conclusion

One or two sentences stating what the file supports and what it does not, in plain language a supervising attorney can act on without reading further.

Exposure Evidence

What is confirmed, what is inferred, and what remains unverified.

Injury Verification

The objective evidence supporting the claimed injury, and any gap between what is claimed and what is documented.

Causation Strengths

The specific factors supporting the causation theory, drawn from the causation mapping pillar.

Competing Causes

Baseline risk factors, alternative explanations, and intervening events — stated honestly, not minimized.

Defense Vulnerabilities

What a well-prepared defense is likely to argue, based on the adversarial review discipline described in Chapter 29.

Missing Evidence

Anything still outstanding that could change the classification.

Expert Needs

Whether expert referral is warranted, and if so, the specific question the referral should pose.

Recommended Attorney Action

The action called for under the Attorney Decision Matrix, stated as a next step, not a restatement of the classification.

Appendix O — Missing Evidence and Discovery Crosswalk

For each category of missing evidence identified during record integrity review, this crosswalk should record: what is missing, why it matters to the claim, who is likely to hold it, the discovery device or collection pathway most likely to obtain it (authorization, subpoena, request for production, deposition), and what decision — classification, expert referral, settlement posture — depends on receiving it. A firm maintaining this crosswalk consistently should be able to look at any missing-record finding and immediately identify the correct next step, rather than treating each gap as a fresh research question.

Appendix P — Claimant Interview and Exposure Verification Guide

Interview questions should ask specifically about brand, product, frequency, duration, dose, location of use, treating or prescribing provider, and purchase or acquisition history — general questions produce general answers that do not hold up once the record integrity review begins. Questions should be open-ended and non-leading; a claimant's account is more useful, and more defensible later, when it comes from their own recollection than from a question that supplied the answer.

Corroboration Hierarchy

For any claimant statement bearing on exposure, rank the available corroboration from strongest to weakest: contemporaneous medical or pharmacy records; contemporaneous non-medical records (purchase receipts, employment records); corroborating witness statements from someone with independent knowledge; and, at the base of the hierarchy, the claimant's own recollection alone, unsupported by any record.

Contradiction Protocol

When a claimant's account changes between intake and a later interview, or conflicts with a record once obtained, document both versions, the date each was given, and — where possible — a plausible explanation grounded in the record rather than an assumption about the claimant's credibility. Reconciling the conflict, not concealing it, is the goal; an unaddressed contradiction discovered by the defense is far more damaging than the same contradiction the firm has already accounted for.

Affidavit Cautions

Exposure affidavits should reflect what the claimant actually recalls, not a level of precision the claimant's memory does not support. Manufacturing false precision — a specific date, a specific frequency — that the claimant did not actually supply creates a sworn statement the record may later contradict. Where a record can establish the same fact more reliably than memory, cite the record instead of asking the claimant to swear to a detail they are reconstructing rather than recalling.

Appendix Q — Expert Referral Package

A complete referral package, built from the litigation-ready output described in Chapter 12 and the referral discipline in Chapter 27, should include: the specific, pre-framed question the expert is being asked to answer, rather than a general request to review the file; the completed causation map from Appendix H or its claimant-specific equivalent; the sequenced imaging findings, where imaging is relevant; the reconstructed timeline; the baseline profile and identified competing causes; the record integrity audit showing what has and has not been obtained; and the defense-vulnerability analysis from the firm's own adversarial review, so the expert is working from a file that already reflects what the opposing side is likely to argue. A referral package this complete is what separates an expert opinion built to withstand cross-examination from one that simply restates the chronology.

Appendix R — Defense Challenge Checklist

This is a completed adversarial-review template, not merely a description of the exercise in Chapter 29. For each claimant selected for advanced review, an independent reviewer — someone who did not build the claimant's original classification — should work through and document a position on each of the following: alternative causation grounded in the claimant's own documented history; pre-existing disease predating the exposure period; insufficient or absent proof of actual exposure; dose or duration too limited to plausibly cause the claimed injury; latency inconsistent with the exposure-injury relationship; diagnoses not well supported by objective findings; imaging that conflicts with the claimed injury; intervening events complicating the causal chain; documented treatment noncompliance; injuries or symptoms arising after the exposure period; inconsistent or unsupported damages claims; and, where applicable, genuine scientific uncertainty about the underlying exposure-injury relationship. For each item, record whether the concern applies to this claimant, and if so, whether the existing record resolves it, requires further investigation, or remains a genuine, unresolved vulnerability.

Appendix S — Clinical Intelligence Issue Log

For any open question, contradiction, or unresolved finding surfaced during review, this log should record: the issue itself, stated specifically; the source or record that raised it; the confidence level associated with the current understanding of the issue; any contradicting evidence on file; the specific open question that remains; the person responsible for resolving it; a due date; and, once resolved, the resolution and the record that resolved it. Maintaining this log separately from the claimant's narrative file keeps open questions visible and assigned, rather than buried in prose a reviewer has to reread to rediscover what is still unresolved.

Appendix T — Version and Reclassification Log

Every classification recorded in the firm's system should be tied to the version of the classification framework in effect at the time, per the discipline described in Chapter 34. This log operationalizes that requirement at the claimant level: for each claimant, record the classification assigned, the framework version it was assigned under, the date, the specific finding or evidence that produced this classification, and — for any subsequent reclassification — the prior classification, what changed, and why. A firm that can produce this history for any claimant on request is in a materially stronger position, both internally and if the firm's review process itself is ever challenged, than one that can only show its current, final answer.

Appendix U — General-to-Specific Causation Alignment Worksheet

For each claimant, record the operative general-causation proposition the litigation has adopted, the claimant-specific evidence bearing on that proposition, the factors supporting alignment between the two, the factors conflicting with that alignment, the specific question this raises for the retained expert, and any gap that remains unresolved. This worksheet exists to surface, early and explicitly, any place where a claimant's specific evidence does not comfortably fit the general-causation theory the firm has adopted — exactly the kind of conflict Part VIII identifies as needing to surface before the expert encounters it, not after.

About the Author

Michelle Carroll is the Founder and CEO of Lexcura Summit, a medical-legal analysis firm built around Clinical Intelligence, a discipline she developed to bring clinical rigor to legal case evaluation. She is the author of five previously published books on medical-legal analysis and has contributed papers to the American Health Law Association (AHLA). Her work focuses on helping attorneys and firms evaluate the clinical strength of complex litigation before committing significant time and resources, replacing assumption-driven case selection with evidence-based analysis. She founded Lexcura Summit to bring this methodology to firms handling medically complex litigation at scale, including through the training and licensing program described in this book.

www.ingramcontent.com/pod-product-compliance
Lightning Source LLC
LaVergne TN
LVHW051134210926
848482LV00006B/316